The CEO'S COMPASS:

YOUR GUIDE TO GET BACK ON TRACK

By
Deborah A. Coviello

The CEO's Compass
Your guide to get back on track
by Deborah A. Coviello
Copyright © 2021 Deborah A. Coviello
Published by SkillBites LLC
https://skillbites.net/
All rights reserved.

ISBN-13: 978-1-952281-43-3 paperback
ISBN-13: 978-1-952281-44-0 eBook

Testimonials

I had the opportunity to observe some of Deborah's journey over the past couple of years. In *The CEO's Compass*, she captures insights, wisdom, and inspiration from her own experience as well as from various leaders and experts. A great example of what can be accomplished with determination and the confidence to push ahead. Anyone reading this book will find gems and nuggets to help guide them in their own journey. As the saying goes: "A rising tide lifts all boats."

-**Germain St. Denis**, The Architect of People First, Toronto, Canada

High performers are destined to get trapped by their own success and eventually fall adrift. *The CEO's Compass* offers a framework to get back on course by an expert practitioner who has been there and done that time after time.

This book is packed with useful insight, tactics, and loving nudges. Deb reminds us that we often know the answers to our problems but we allow ourselves to get in our own way. Let the CEO's Compass point you back in the right direction so you can start conquering the world again.

-**Nick Smith,** Chairman of the Board at Winton Place Youth Center and Founder of the Innopreneur Podcast, Ohio, US

I am always honored to be invited to join Deb on her podcasts. She is one of the most enlightening and thought-provoking individuals that I know! Her book is sure to help people self-reflect and ultimately become more successful!

-**Lou Tutino,** Executive Recruiter, Florida, US

A compass is a gift that most never appreciate until it is firmly in their hands. It removes ambiguity and enables those who use it to see a clearer way forward, where without it, all they see is chaos and confusion.

Thanks for providing the world with *The CEO's Compass*. Each CEO who touches this will steer their ships that much straighter because of it and reach their goals that much easier.

-**Ben Baker,** www.yourbrandmarketing.com, British Columbia, Canada

If you have ever wanted someone to coach you through what it takes to lead yourself and your team, then *The CEO's Compass* is for you. Author Deb Coviello walks readers through the phases of understanding themself and their capabilities, building on those resources, and then standing up to lead others. Coviello, who began her career as an engineer before becoming a Human Resources consultant, knows of what she writes. She has lived it and, fortunately for us, is able to share her insights in ways that resonate with practicality and wisdom.

-**John Baldoni,** member of Marshall Goldsmith 100 Coaches and author of 15 books on leadership, including his newest, *Grace Notes: Leading in an Upside-Down World*, Michigan, US

'In this excellent book, Deborah A. Coviello offers incredibly valuable practical leadership lessons and tools for leaders at all levels. *The CEO's Compass* provides you the framework for peace of mind and includes tactical points aligned with people, processes, and platforms.'

-**Dr. Oleg Konovalov,** global thought leader, author of *The Vision Code*, the da Vinci of visionary leadership, Moscow, Russia

"Leadership is hard. Leading others requires experience, empathy, vision, and persistence. In her new book, *The CEO's Compass*, Deb Coviello provides a terrific model to which leaders can defer in order to lead and change effectively. I especially love the "peace of mind" component of the model, as all employees need their leaders to have a clear view of the future and approach that future positively and effectively. I also love the "people" component, as a great leader knows his/her most significant assets in order to achieve the future are his/her people. Net/net, the whole model is a great way to think about leadership."

-**Ed Evarts,** Leadership and Team Coach, Business Strategist, Author and Podcaster, Excellius Leadership Development, Massachusetts, US

When you are facing a major challenge as the CEO that you have never encountered before and you don't know how you are going to solve it, you have two choices: succeed or be succeeded. Being the chief decision maker at this point can feel very lonely. Not only do you know that you are off track but you know you have a limited window to get back on track.

The CEO's Compass is the perfect guide to help you think through the strategies and tactics that will be most important to get you past roadblocks like these. With her remarkable experience as a leader and as a guide to leaders, Deb Coviello provides a unique set of insights and a roadmap that will give you the peace of mind to know that "you've got this."

-**David Shriner-Cahn,** Host, Smashing the Plateau
& Going Solo, New York, US

The CEO's Compass is a must have for any leader—especially for one who looks at their role and responsibilities beyond the desk. Deborah's powerful focus on legacy, chaos, survival, and teamwork has inspired me to rethink my work with others. Audiences connect with my calls for the "Herculean Effort" needed by everyone from the farm to the fork—an enormous amount of work, strength, and courage to speak up and act at all times to keep our food safe. When we elevate the personal impact of an individual, we bring out the superhero in all of us!

-**Dr. Darin Detwiler,** Founder and CEO of Detwiler
Consulting Group, LLC., Keynote Speaker, Professor,
and Author of *FOOD SAFETY: Past, Present,
and Predictions*, Los Angeles, US

Deb Coviello exemplifies what is so desperately needed in these confusing and conflicted times: a splendid balance of professional experience, business acumen, and ethical courage. *The CEO's Compass* should provide leaders with a valuable tool for creating a purpose-driven culture, finding clarity amidst chaos, and cultivating a mindset for success and prosperity.

-**Yonason Goldson**
Author of *Grappling with the Gray* and co-host of
The Rabbi and the Shrink, Missouri, US

Table of Contents

Acknowledgements.. ix

Dedication xi

Foreword xiii

Chapter 1:   It's Personal: What Changed and
             why are You off Track? 1

Chapter 2:   I'm Your Partner: Why am I Writing this
             Book for You? 7

Chapter 3:   Compass Point: Peace of Mind and
             Finding Your True North...............................17

Chapter 4:   Compass Point: Purpose 29

Chapter 5:   Compass Point: The Past, Skipping the
             Past is a Recipe for Failure...........................45

Chapter 6:   Compass Point: Pride, The Intersection
             of Humanity and Intellectual Property...........55

Chapter 7:   Compass Point: People, People are
             the Greatest Tool in Your Toolbox 65

Chapter 8:   Compass Point: Process, The Fairy-Tale—
             PDCA & DMAIC Don't Fix a Process..............83

Chapter 9:   Compass Point: Platform Tools that
             Elevate Your Team's Impact 97

Chapter 10: Compass Point: Performance 111

Chapter 11: The CEO's Compass: How The System
             Works Together...125

Chapter 12: Leaving a Lasting Impact and Handing
             the Compass to Your Team 135

About the Author 139

Acknowledgements

You all left an impact on me and are recognized in no particular order

Amanda Lund—for helping me to push to my limits and find my brand voice.

Jennifer DiMenna—found my brand image and helped me show up as the Drop-In CEO

Karyl Eckerle—for helping me to bring my brand image forward with confidence.

Judy Weintraub—my book guide who helped me to navigate a large ocean while maintaining calm waters.

Peter Goral—who helped me to get over myself and gently nudged me along my journey. He is a mentor, a friend, and an amazing human.

Dave Haase—who just wanted to see me succeed and offered me endless mentorship.

Mario Porreca—who helped me to find the Drop-In CEO. Your amazing podcast *10 Minute Mindset* was the inspiration for creating *The Drop-In CEO* podcast.

Jack Kahler—for trusting me to fly wingman on a consulting assignment and teaching me the ropes when I was still so green.

Jeffrey Shaw—who influenced me through his podcast, *The Self-Employed Life,* and his book *Lingo.* He helped me to believe in myself and create Illumination Partners.

Margie Warrell—whose book *Brave* was one of the inspirations for the realization that I could create my own business.

Dorie Clark—whose three books *Stand Out*, *Reinventing You*, and *Entrepreneurial You* all influenced me to start a business and to "stand out."

Mom—for always having my back and being one of my biggest fans! I hear you cheering and ringing the bell for me.

Dedication

To my husband Dan—my best friend who puts up with my early morning chats, kicks me in the butt when I get off track, and lives to see my eyes roll when he cracks a joke. You were truly the one who said "you can be a CEO" when I could not see it myself. If only I had listened to you sooner, who knows where I'd be now. The *CEO's Compass* is the beginning of the journey, and I can't wait to see where it takes us and everyone who reads it.

Foreword

How can reading *The CEO's Compass* help you and the people who are important to you have better lives? This is a key question I urge you to keep in mind as you read this book.

If I have learned one thing in my life, it's the fact that everyone wants to be appreciated. This goes for CEO's and managers as well as employees; parents as well as children. We never outgrow this need. The fact is we need others to help us feel valued.

Throughout this book, Deb provides you with key points that will help you get your organization back on track and reach "peace of mind." For me, it was realizing I was not alone in facing the challenge of major change in my company. I had to trust my people, and they had to trust me. However, getting there can be challenging for many leaders.

If you are feeling like the burden of change is on your shoulders, then this book is for you. Deb will walk you through the process that best fits your organization. With the right tools, the job will get easier.

Never be too proud to ask for help, even if it is from a book. I read a quote many years ago that resonates with me to this day: "I use all the brain I have and all that I can borrow!"

I urge you to do something special for others and yourself—incorporate The CEO's Compass into your life.

Dave Haase

Retired Vice President at Mane

You are my Transition Hero and I Wrote this Book for You

You are my Transition Hero and I dedicate this book and well-placed questions to you. This book was designed to share the insights that I've gathered throughout my career and to inspire you to find answers to understand why you are off track. I do want to be clear that the book is not a "how to succeed in 5 steps" instruction manual as many authors have written, claiming to solve your problems. That model does not serve you as a leader. Leaders seek insights and data around them and find the inspiration within themselves to get back on track. *The CEO's Compass* is your navigation tool to assess where you are off track and identify the course corrections you can easily take yourself. It is also meant to make you think before you take action. A leader's greatest strength is knowing when to pause, reflect and be inspired rather than influenced by others. Delivering this book Is something I never would have done in my prior life, but having a deep need to connect with you was my impetus to create. It was the driving force to provide a platform to inspire your thoughts and get you back on track. This book is not a magic bullet, but in the framework of this compass is the help you need to find your true north—it's already within you. You simply need a guide.

As this story unfolds in front of you, you will find the nuggets of insight to inspire you to do something different. That is the Drop-In CEO brand of inspiring you to achieve your goals. I'm simply your support system. So, let's get started!

Having clarity amidst chaos
cuts through the noise.

CHAPTER 1

It's Personal: What Changed and why are You off Track?

I see you. I see you staring out the window wondering how you are going to meet this challenge. You're thinking to yourself that you're smart, you're tough, and you've gotten through bigger challenges than this, but you find yourself unable to get past this obstacle. You start to doubt your abilities, asking yourself if you are cut out for this work anymore. Maybe it's time to explore new opportunities, maybe take a vacation, but none of this is possible because in the moment … you're stuck. There's nowhere to go but to face the storm head-on, although you don't know what to do next.

This realization is tough for you because you reflect back to the days when you were a "rock star" whose high performance landed you in the role you have now. You went in with high hopes. Maybe things had been going well for many years, but then the environment changed. We know conditions change all the time; it's your past skills that elevated you to every challenge in life and business, and that's why you are the right person for the role. But you're questioning yourself now: why you can't get through this one? What's different, and what new skills do you need to elevate yourself to rock-star status again?

While the beginning of this story starts in a place that can be lonely and unsettling, there is a way out. I was you once— well, maybe several times—and it's very uncomfortable when we hit new lows. We all know these times are what makes us stronger as we intellectualize what we're going through. However, we often find we have limited skills and support systems to get us through these challenges we've never been faced with before.

Challenges are what make us better as humans and what elevate our skills. For the right person at the right time, with a little self-awareness, you can rise above and become even better than you were before—but only if you're ready. If you're still reading this first chapter, you may be one of those people who are ready, but are not convinced a book is going to help you. Your situation is unique, and people are depending on you to find a solution. You have prided yourself on doing things alone and know intellectually that a book is not the answer.

However, I need you to pause and reflect because the intellectualization of your current situation is not going to serve you going forward. Maybe starting from a place of thinking versus doing might get you a different result. What was rewarded in the past for being a quick thinker and react-ing to circumstances has become exhausting. You need a different plan, system, or support that moves the ship in a different direction and, more importantly, provides clarity amidst chaos.

Clarity amidst chaos—what do I mean by that? I mean being able to think clearly, see the bigger challenges and opportunities, and create a course that pulls you in a direction that is proactive instead of reactive. It's about taking control of how you navigate any challenges and perhaps avoid them in the future because you can see the big picture. It is that moment in time where you can see, think, and hear clearly. It is that deep breath during which you can feel the air clearing your mind.

I need you to take a deep breath and think about how you feel. I've learned that taking the time to simply acknowledge the energy you are feeling in your mind and body is one way of taking time for you. Not clearing your mind and quieting how you feel will not serve you. Think about what calms your mind. Is it reading a book, taking a walk, closing your eyes and nodding off, cooking, or perhaps exercise? I need you to schedule some of that time for yourself and put this book down. Come back when you are in a calmer place and not thinking about your current challenge.

I have found that quieting how you feel and relieving some of the stress is the first step in taking the time to think and be open to new ideas about your challenges. By the way, we don't start with the challenge you have in front of you—we start from a place of understanding how you feel and what guides you. We need to go back to the core of who you are and what has provided you success in the past. We need to embrace who you are and bring you back to a place of realizing your gifts and talents before moving forward. Only when you start by pausing and reflecting about yourself can you start the journey again and provide yourself with the compass to guide you on a different path.

The compass is my gift to you because I care about you. I understand the career challenges both firsthand and from seeing it in the eyes of the clients in front of me. I see your self-determination, but I also feel your doubt and stress. The CEO feels it stronger than anyone but because of the title "CEO" has to put on a façade. You may or may not have a CEO's title, but you are the head of a large entity or organization and have top-line accountability, and you need to succeed. It's about succeeding or be succeeded; no room for a performance improvement plan.

The compass is simply a tool that helps you find the direction you need to take. What makes the compass different from someone else's five-step plan is that you find all the answers versus being given a solution. When you give yourself the time and space to think and come to your own conclusions, the results are far more successful and sustainable. You regain command of who you are and how you serve those who have elevated you to your leadership role. You regain your confidence because you do not have to change yourself, you simply have to find your compass to lead others through the challenge. New challenges will come all the time, but reverting back to simple navigation tools will guide you.

If you are at a point where you need support, a guide, and a compass, I ask that you put this book down to simply pause and reflect. Reflect on whether you are ready to trust yourself, think for yourself, and learn a few new things about yourself and how you interface with the world. If the answer is yes, commit to picking up this book tomorrow and reading the next chapter.

This book is not a quick fix, and it is not meant to be read too quickly. It's meant to get you to slow down and reflect. Take each chapter and sub-chapter and give yourself permission to pause and reflect on how each insight is relevant to your situation. Trust yourself and the process of going on this journey with yourself and then with the CEO's compass. When you, like a captain of a ship, can trust your compass to get through a storm, people around you will see this and trust you when the next challenge arises. I promise you that. Take a look at the questions below and internalize them. Absorb them with your mind and pick just one or two that pertain to you.

- What keeps you up at night? What worries you?
- Are you confident in yourself? How do you show this?
- Are you confident you have the capability and capacity to achieve your goals?
- What do you think is missing? Is it your self-confidence or your ability to achieve your goals? What support do you need?

CHAPTER 2

I'm Your Partner:
Why am I Writing this Book for You?

As the CEO or business leader in your company, until now, you've been highly successful. You've gotten to where you have because of your leadership and your ability to make a difference and leave a lasting impact. And then something changed. You've lost your way. You're having problems. And you're not sure where to go, whom to turn to address the challenges you're facing.

You could be having issues with quality, service, profitability, resources; the list goes on and on. I've seen all of that. And in Chapter One, we talked about you: how I see you, how I can serve you as we journey into rough waters together, and how I can guide you through using the compass. Today I'm your partner because I've also been there as a leader.

In my previous roles as the head of quality for a multinational organization and as the head of operational excellence,

I, too, have been that highly experienced leader dropped into a chaotic situation, who had to transform in order to be able to bring the organization into the calm waters on the other side.

I know you're looking for stability. You're looking for that something that will get you back to True North and peace of mind. Before I share the details of the CEO's compass, I want to share a letter that I've written to you and all the CEOs and business owners who have lost their way.

Dear CEO or Business Leader:

We have not met yet, so let me introduce myself. I'm Deb Coviello, founder of Illumination Partners. I simply want to reach out to learn more about you: what excites you, what is your business, what is your amazing past, and what are you most proud of?

I love to hear these stories, and I simply want to build a meaningful relationship with you. It's because I've worked in so many similar businesses that I know both the challenges and aspirations, and I would simply love to be your partner. You see, when you share your business aspirations with me, I can see the future where we really need to take you and your business.

I have that expertise in quality, continuous improvement, problem-solving, and leadership development. More importantly, I can also drop into your organization and be your partner to navigate the changes and challenges you're experiencing. As the "Drop-In CEO," we work together. I become part of your strategy to move your organization through the challenge, elevate your team during the process, and ultimately bring you peace of mind.

I know peace of mind is very private and personal and sometimes hard to describe However, once you have found your true north leveraging the compass points as your guide, when you arrive, you will know it. You will have achieved great results. You will feel passionate, you will be leveraging your strengths, and you will lead your team for lasting impact.

Just know that I can simply be a sounding board to frame what the future looks like. My abilities lie in reframing what you've said into a strategic outcome that provides you peace of mind and will bring you great comfort. I become a partner who not only takes care of short-term business challenges but also has a way of bringing out the best in you and your people for sustainable growth.

So, having said that, I would love to have a conversation with you. But until we meet and have this conversation, I offer you the CEO's Compass. It is my approach to getting you back on track. Please accept this book as my gift to you, and I sincerely hope you enjoy the journey, select the points that suit you best, and remember to keep it in your pocket for when you need to get back on track.

Sincerely,

Deborah A. Coviello

Founder of Illumination Partners, LLC and The Drop-In CEO

Now let's just talk about a few more things as we start bringing you into the story. Again, I do this work simply because I want to help you. And yes, obviously we want to personally achieve great results, but I find the greatest satisfaction in being able to help not only solve your business problem but also leave a lasting impact. And let me be clear. It's not about me: it's all about you.

Everything I do is about you and your team, and the work that we will do together is about leaving that lasting impact. I will share a few stories because you don't have to believe me. You could believe the stories of the people who have worked with me.

Leaving your Legacy

I have one particular colleague from the flavors industry. When I left that organization, they said, "Deb, you're everywhere. I see the work that you've done. You've left your mark on this organization. Now, when people speak about quality and continuous improvement, they still speak the language as if you were still here."

So, we leave a lasting impact. That's the kind of work that I can do with you. But I want to share another story. And again, this is how I partner with you.

Clarity Amidst Chaos

A VP of operations was in the midst of a high-profile quality issue. They knew they were going to be potentially shifting the organization in a way that would impact people's lives, who would perhaps even lose their jobs. There was also the chance that they would lose a senior leader in their organization.

Talk about going through change! While they were quite capable and had tremendous leadership skills, they were still challenged. When I was able to reframe the problem and identify the fact that they probably needed a drop-in interim leader, they became calm. I shared with them that I could partner with them and deal with these challenges of quality amid downsizing. I could be that interim leadership and, in the process, we could elevate the team and leave them with the skills they needed for the future. Once I shared that, the leader nodded and nodded again, and closed their eyes. I could see that I was getting to the core of what was bothering them, and that's the relationship that we can have together.

Remaining Relevant to Survive

And finally, just one more client I want to share with you. I love the clients whom I work with. This person doesn't give testimonials. This person doesn't tell me "I love the work that you've done. You've given me peace of mind." It's their actions that show me I'm their partner and I'm going to help them.

I helped them to maintain their quality certification as a requirement for a customer to remain on their core supplier list. After they received this certification, I didn't hear from them for several months. Then I got a text message: "Deb, I need your help. I have this challenge. Can you help me with an environmental health and safety program?"

I said "Sure. I can help you, but I've never done this before." Then they came back and said, "We'll learn together!" And this is what leaving a lasting impact looks like. It's about that trust. It's that relationship. It's what we build together. It's not just the problem that we solve, but the relationship we develop that leaves a lasting impact.

Let's get back to you and how my experience can be distilled into a single system. While most consultants have their three-step, five-step, even ten-step approaches, it is my belief that every business has different strengths and weaknesses and not everything has to get fixed—instead, slight course corrections are usually enough.

The CEO's Compass does indeed have eight points that you can select from to get on track wherever you need to make those adjustments. It is also important to know that using a few of the points in combination with others can not only get you back on track but set your direction for sustainable impact and peace of mind.

When we work together, we look at the best of your organization and continue to leverage that which has brought you great success. We look at where you're off track and make minor course corrections to get you back on track for sustainable results while lifting the capability of the people on your team. The CEO's Compass has its foundation in human-centric points for which solving technical issues through developing your individual and team performance is critical to success. This book is a tool to assess where you are off track and where you need to make changes.

I am a consultant when you get down to it, but I'm the Drop-in CEO, which is a mindset. It's my ability to understand you. While I haven't been a CEO in title, that really doesn't matter. What really matters is my ability to see you, understand you, and help guide you back on track.

Stepping Back to Assess What Is Needed

When you look at an organization that is no longer performing, it can be addressed in both an emotional way and a tactical way. I will start with the tactical, because that is the tried-and-true way of solving problems and addressing pain points. As an example, if you have had a quality issue trending upward over time, it has probably made your customers angry enough that they're threatening to leave you. That is a pain point. We get together our process improvement teams. We try to find the root cause, we analyze data, and we implement improvement activities. We see the trend reverse. We high-five: we're back on track and we can breathe easy. But I ask you, have you achieved peace of mind or only temporarily put the problem aside?

Sometimes we can be very tactical. We can fix people. We can fix processes. We can even throw tools and techniques around, and get people certified, and implement ERP systems, et cetera. We can absolutely solve tactical business problems, but does this sustainably address the problem?

That's where I challenge you to think differently. I want you to think about the essential skills of an organization; the emotional side of your business. I know sometimes people don't like to hear this, but as your partner—and I am your partner—I'm going to say things to you that you may not want to hear.

You need to take care of people, hence my human-centric leadership style. The CEO's Compass includes tactical points aligned with people, processes, and platforms (tools), which we will treat as tactical directions. I propose to you that we shift how you think about people, processes, and platforms to an emotional perspective. We'll go into this at a deeper level in later chapters.

You also need to understand the people on your team, their pasts and their cultures, because that will help you understand the human dynamics when they come together—when you're solving tactical problems.

I also suggest you understand pride. The pride of the people is critical. My definition of "pride" is unique: pride is the intersection of the person, their intellectual property, and the gifts that they bring forward. Leaders need to take time to understand the pride that people carry and bring that forward sooner than later.

Invest in Mentoring or People Become an Expense

As a leader, your role is to elevate your people and ensure they have the essential skills to follow your lead and become thinkers as well as doers. You need to provide a framework to give your people feedback, build their confidence, understand them, and enhance their mindset to be able to serve you.

We go into this in much greater detail in later chapters, but because it's a significant compass point, we need to spend some time now to set the stage. If you have the right people with the right skills on the team within a framework that mentors, coaches, and supports them, those people are going to take care of you. Serve the people and serve the teams and you'll build a lasting impact as you get back on track.

Every compass point we speak about includes a human element, and because this is so critical, it also has its own compass point. When people see that you lead with a human-centric approach, they'll open their minds, they'll learn new things, they'll start to bring ideas to the table, and they'll perform at levels much higher than they would in traditional systems. The beauty of the CEO's compass is that it's a tool and guide that will last you a lifetime.

Put it away when you're on track. Take it out when you need a course correction. Show your people your compass, and let them know where you're going and which points you're choosing. They may suggest different directions based on the destination they see, and together the team will rise to take care of the navigation, finding true north and peace of mind.

This book is the culmination of my insights and those I've learned from others. If you understand the basic concept, you can stop here. But if you're curious about my insight about the compass, the pain points that can show you you're not on track, my assessment techniques, and specific tools that you can use, I ask that you continue reading.

I can help you leave a lasting impact. And it is my hope that when you're done reading this chapter, you will continue onto the next one, and the next one. Read the actionable tips that I'm going to share with you in every chapter, and you can start steering the ship back on course yourself. That's my gift for you.

However, remember I can also be your partner to drive this journey together. I do look forward to speaking to you someday to get your feedback on this book and if it was helpful. Maybe you found a new compass point and we can evolve the tool together.

I sincerely want to thank you for staying with me through this chapter, if for nothing else than to become acquainted with each other. I love engaging in conversation, building a relationship with you, exchanging ideas, and moving forward together. As one mentor said to me, "All I want to see is you succeed!"

If our journey together stops here, I simply want to wish you continued success and maybe our ships will cross in the future.

And now the rest of the story ...

Throughout my life, I've often felt a little off course, always trying to find the compass that would get me back on track. It was during a reflective moment that I realized that all I needed to navigate to where I had peace of mind was inside of me; I simply needed the courage to find it and trust its guidance.

I share with you this short poem to inspire you and give you the confidence that "you've got this" and we can navigate this journey together.

Look back and Learn
Look inside and Feel
Look forward and Lead
Look up and Thank
Look around and Unite
Look across and Join
Look in the mirror and be You

CHAPTER 3

Compass Point: Peace of Mind and Finding Your True North

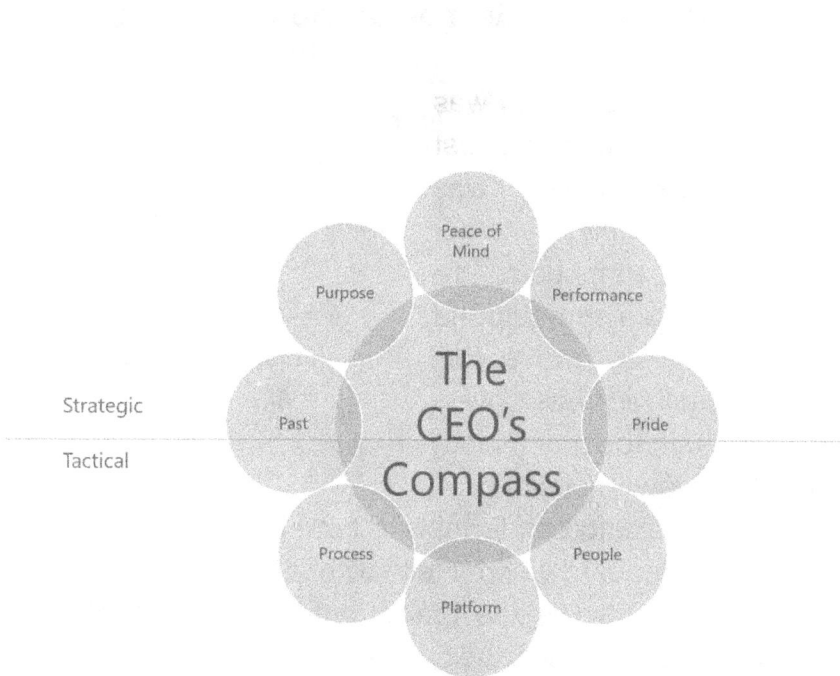

This is my favorite compass point because it is the ultimate outcome we seek when we're not on track. Peace of mind is something that you must define for yourself, but you know it when you have it. It's that state of being where your needs are met and you can truly enjoy the fruits of your efforts. It comes with that smell of fresh air on a cold crisp day. It comes when you see your child wave goodbye as they step onto the college campus and start the rest of their life. It's knowing your financial needs are met. It's knowing you've led a good life and can now leave your legacy to others. Sure, we can probably create a measurable scale to demonstrate where you are on that spectrum, but let's keep it simple for now. You know it when you feel it; it's emotional and very personal.

Being Off Course, but Knowing that the Compass Will Guide You in the Right Direction

Let me start by saying, I was writing this book in my last role without knowing it. I was in crisis, and only my engineering and continuous improvement training equipped me to tactically move forward. When I was overwhelmed with too much input and too few solutions, I

> *When your mind is blank and you can't create content, embrace it! An artist must start with a blank canvas!*

moved from sitting comfortably in front of my computer and onto the whiteboard where I felt vulnerable.

The whiteboard is the brainstorming tool of choice for teams that want to see their work, but as an engineer, I reverted to my computer where my thoughts were private. Knowing that past strengths were not going to serve me moving forward, I threw my faith into putting my ideas on a whiteboard and asking others what they thought about my concepts.

My region was in the last place in quality out of four regions and I had to find a way to move myself and my team forward. The words, phrases, and pictures were disconnected, but I knew my training would be able to draw connections given time and space. At first my team did not understand the disconnected thoughts when I invited them in, but as I explained the pieces it gave them clarity and they grew able to contribute. While I felt vulnerable, there was comfort in having my team contributing to the outcome. The process of getting my thoughts out in the open before aligning and organizing them provided me the ability to move toward peace of mind. It enabled me to move from the tactical frenzy of fighting fires to a strategic purpose and mindful, well-thought-out work. It also provided my team the ability to create a roadmap for their work and to move their functions forward.

The effort in this story I share with you did not provide peace of mind unto itself, but it did provide purpose and the levers to pull to achieve the ultimate outcome. However, the ability for you as a leader to simply pause, reflect, and bring forward your thoughts is the first step in achieving peace of mind. It starts and ends with you, and unless you break through and plan your course, you'll never get there.

I'll continue this story in subsequent chapters, because it was the genesis of the CEO's Compass. Now, let me share with you an example of what peace of mind looks like in business.

Leadership in Crisis

I was face to face with a senior leader in crisis, facing a plant closure, a product recall, and no senior leadership in the quality department to manage these challenges. I could see the frustration and frenzy both in their words and in their body language. As I listened to their challenge and processed how I might help them, I shared the following: "You need a senior leader who can manage the technical issues to resolution. You need to ensure the business is sustainable through the transition. You need assurance that you can maintain customer brand loyalty." As soon as I shared that summary with the leader to show I understood the challenge and the outcome they needed, their body instantly relaxed and centered. They simply said "Yes" with a deep and soulful sigh. I could see peace of mind coming forward onto their face as they trusted me and were confident I could get them on the right track.

Another observation I've made in my personal experiences is that peace of mind is not always achievable right away. A senior leader must weather the storm of crisis and move people out of inefficient and ineffective activities to a place where they're working in sync with each other toward a common goal. The leader needs to take on the pressure internally and provide a calm framework in which the people on their team can do productive work and come out on the other side to a place of stability, out of crisis, where they can all heave a sigh of relief.

There is one caveat here I must impress upon you. Peace of mind is not getting through the crisis and then high-five, we made it through another day. I know you've had those days, hoping you could forget the crisis you were just in. A leader needs to acknowledge that until we've gotten to the root cause of the crisis, it will rear its ugly head again. Before offering some actionable tips for you, I'd like to share a personal story that may demonstrate how your leadership is critical to peace of mind for your team.

Teams in Crisis—Multiple Crises!

"Deb, can I talk to you?" The door to the office closed behind my senior staff employee. The dread of what would come next sent up my internal red flag, but I remained calm with a friendly demeanor and asked how I could help them. "I've been just informed we also have a quality issue at our east coast plant and I propose we go out there immediately to do a deep investigation." I thanked them for their proposal, asked for an update as they planned that effort, and offered my support. I later had to fly out as part of that triage team because it was a smaller plant that lacked the capacity and capability to run the business as well as a deep investigation.

As this crisis was escalating and being managed by my team, I was managing multiple crises in two Midwest plants, both of similar urgency. As these issues were mounting, I was tactically deploying resources and managing the efforts, but inside, my tension was rising and my confidence was sinking. I knew I had the tactical expertise to manage through the crisis, but not much bandwidth to understand the root cause and how I had arrived at this point in time. The team never saw this doubt, but it was clear I was not on course for true north anymore. I clearly needed to look at my compass and determine which direction to go.

While I was trying to figure out both the tactical crisis and find my true north, another employee came to talk to me. They simply wanted to talk through their role in supporting these efforts, clarify their actions, and receive direction. When we were done, they remarked to me: "You have a way of staying calm during these crises despite how daunting they may be." That statement was so powerful to hear as a leader because being the true north for your team even when you're in chaos provides them peace of mind. When they know you are taking care of them because you give the impression of calm waters, you give them confidence. When your team has confidence, they will take care of the challenging work until the crisis is over.

The point I want to make for you is that it is critical for you to show peace of mind to your team while you're in the process of getting there yourself. You need your team focused to get through the crisis while you look further into the future to sustain the peace of mind for both your team and yourself.

Peace of Mind for You

What I'm about to share with you may not surprise you, but I offer you no silver bullets to achieve peace of mind. There, I've said it! It may disappoint you that I've not provided you what you were looking for, but please stay with me. It's about you and defining what peace of mind looks like for you, which can only happen if you put down this book and simply pause. Stop reading and consuming, start feeling and thinking. I know life coaches suggest you should have morning routines, reflect on what you're grateful for, and have a healthy breakfast or exercise to build energy for the day ahead.

Those morning routines (or any time-of-day routines) are useless unless there is intentionality with what you do with your valuable time. I want you to take a moment for yourself and take inventory of how you feel. Do you sigh a lot? Do you have a hard time sleeping? Is your mind always racing? Do you busy yourself all day long with deadlines and meetings, but feel no sense of accomplishment at the end of the day?

Do you have nothing to offer your friends and family at the end of the day except thankless activity?

Now think about a time when you were excited about an activity that energized you every time you engaged with it. Was it a woodworking project, making a quilt, hiking in the woods, watching a child sleep, seeing your favorite sports team win? How did these moments feel? I want you to close your eyes and think about those moments. They may even give you joy. You may shed a tear. You may even sigh again, knowing that peace of mind is something you've felt in your life. But you don't feel it in the work you do and how you lead.

I'll Go First and Share What Peace of Mind Feels Like for Me

This book is for you, and during the process, I sincerely hope you find that the CEO's compass provides you the frame-work for peace of mind. However, if the concept is difficult to understand, I'll share what it means to me to prompt you and your thoughts.

- Peace of mind is the day my son says, "Mom, you were right" in reference to someone's poor judgment. This shows me that the values we instilled in our children—allowing turmoil to happen during their growth and then their independent thinking—enabled them to come to a value-based decision or statement. This is peace of mind.
- Peace of mind is when your adolescent child has a meltdown and later comes back to apologize for their behavior and understands why they behaved that way. It shows that this person had the courage to express

their feeling, the emotional IQ to understand the impact, and the wisdom to know where they were off track.

- Peace of mind is when that employee/mentee/client says "I was inspired by what you said and now I've made this decision for a change in my career." Knowing that another human thought about what you shared and then was inspired to take the initiative to change — that is peace of mind.

- Peace of mind is knowing you've done everything possible to provide comfort and essential emotional needs for an elderly person in your life. You may not agree or get along with their thoughts and actions, but you have peace of mind knowing that you've done all that you can.

- Peace of mind is knowing you have an emotional support system, a significant other or the means to enjoy your life without worry. Humans and the social ecosystem you've set up enable you to be in a place of calm where you are able to create a lasting impact in this world or others. That is why I'm writing this book for you.

Now it's Your Time—Pause and Reflect

When we compartmentalize emotion away from the tactical work we do, it builds stress in our body and depletes our energy. When we

> *Pause and Reflect; the most important tools you need when you're moving fast!*

give time and space to acknowledge how we are feeling, it can be liberating.

I had moments like this when I was let go from my job and had a few months to think. I ran, I listened to podcasts, I read a lot, I wrote, and I did a lot of thinking. For the first time in my life, I gave myself time to *be*, to *create*, and to *think*. Within those moments, accompanied by music or podcasts, I reached moments of joy and great sadness. I was sad for what I had not allowed myself to be, for the thoughts and creative pursuits I had not allowed myself to chase. I realized great joy in knowing I could do anything I wanted and no one was holding me back except myself. I was finally thinking for myself and gaining clarity while throwing away the chaos. I took time for myself, and now it's your time.

I want you to plan to put this book down; I want you to think in a way that can free your mind and evaluate whether you have peace of mind.

The following questions are for you to consider in no particular order. What is peace of mind? If you are not sure, then skip it and go to some additional questions that may get you there. All I am proposing to you is to pause, reflect on what is missing, and think about how it feels and how you would know if you had it. I suggest you not continue with the book until you've spent at least one minute thinking about this. Then I'll share the tools to getting you back on track.

Having the tools of the CEO's compass points are useless if you've not defined true north or peace of mind. There's no rush to the solutions; they'll be there eventually.

Be honest with yourself as you answer these questions, and when you truly feel or see peace of mind, continue to the next chapters.

Pause and Reflect—The Single Greatest Tool for Understanding Your Peace of Mind

- What gives you peace of mind personally?
- If you know what peace of mind feels like, describe those feelings.
- If you don't know, what would you do to think about it and then come up with the answer?
- What would peace of mind look like for a team you lead?
- If you can define peace of mind, what resources would you need in terms of capability, capacity, or direction to achieve it?
- If you're still struggling with peace of mind, do you have a support person to help you discover what it is?

If the future is unclear, return to your goals and beliefs for clarity. They'll never fail you.

CHAPTER 4

Compass Point: Purpose

While finding your purpose has been written and spoken about at length, I truly wonder if the senior leaders in an organization have sought out what this means or if they have merely accepted what has been developed in conference rooms by others. Do you ever question your purpose? Does it make sense to you or does it all sound like so much business-speak? Which of the following sentences makes more sense to you?

- We strive to be the market leader in our sector by building trust and confidence in our brand partnerships and creating lasting partnerships with our customers.
- Every day is a chance to improve the lives of our associates and customers by engaging in collaborative conversations, innovating products that are sustainable to the environment, and sharing a vision to leave a memorable impact on our consumers.

Which seems more purposeful to you? The first one is typical of what you see in most annual reports and everyone simply falls in line with the words. The second connects humans, emotions, and activity into something that can be visualized by everyone and translated into their own activities. There is a sense of connectedness with the second one that needs to be part of your business, team, and individual purpose statement.

When we ask people to achieve a "result," we only get a completed transaction and a false sense of accomplishment. When we ask people to fulfill a purpose or an outcome, people use their minds and creativity. When we ask people questions about how to achieve an outcome that fulfills a greater calling than simply a result, we open up infinite possibilities. At times, fulfilling a purpose can lead to greater results than telling people "heads down, just achieve the result." As you can see, I'm a bit bitter about this point, but also exhilarated about the possibility to elevate you, your teams, and the organizations you engage with.

You will notice that on the CEO's compass, "purpose" is adjacent to "peace of mind." Often, if all the other compass points are performing well, a slight course correction in the area of purpose (the outcome you want to achieve) will be a quick trip to getting you peace of mind. Let me share a few stories so we're aligned on the difference between attaining peace of mind and simply obtaining a result.

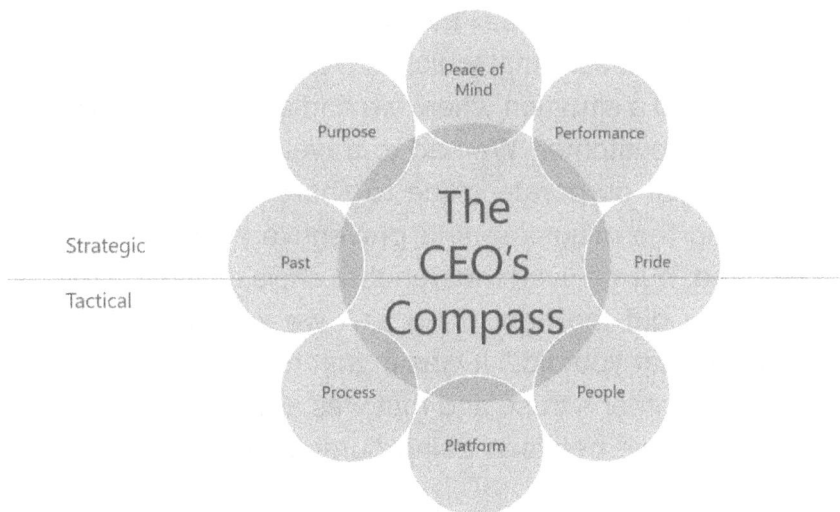

The CEO's Compass

We Know We Should Do Something Different. Some Do and Others Do Not

I once had a colleague who traveled from overseas to learn about the projects in our region as a source of collaboration. I took the opportunity to show them my strategy of leading with a purpose that was aligned to the corporate purpose and then the cascading framework of the strategy down to the tactical work we were doing.

My purpose was simply to be the favorite partner of our customers while enabling our associates to spend more time with their family and doing the things they loved to do. There are two dimensions here that are important to dissect. I did not say I wanted to be number one—I said I wanted to be the favorite. Companies that are "number one" in market share can be toppled by the competition if you measure the relationship in pure numbers. When you measure the relationship by the number of true partnerships on strategic projects, or who the "favorite" is to bail the customer out when they're in trouble, you measure that which leaves a lasting impact.

I once had a situation where we had a very serious quality issue with a customer. We had to travel with our hats in our hands to their corporate office to share the story, the root cause, and the mitigating and preventive actions. We were challenged, but we lived through that crisis only to be told by them, "You did the right thing and we wouldn't change a thing with what you did." It was in that moment I realized we had our customer's trust, and that was all that mattered. This is the difference between being number one and being the favorite.

The other critical dimension is the associates on your team. They work so hard, but do they really need to? I wonder if activity-based management is what drives the quality of life for our team. If we work them until they have nothing left to give their personal life, then there is also no creativity left for the business. In the situation I describe above, knowing I had also worked myself to the bone, I knew we had to find better ways of working, preventing issues, and proactively achieving a better quality of life for our people. When you serve the people, they will take care of the business.

So, back to my colleague who opened this chapter—they were in awe of the quality strategy I had put together to elevate my region and said "I need to do this for my region as well." And so, after that encounter, we parted ways and agreed to stay in touch. They never did create a strategy or purpose statement for their region, yet they met their performance objectives that year. They were in the number two position in quality (as judged by complaints and internal defects), and we were still in fourth.

Fast forward to two years later, my region had moved from fourth to second place, surpassing my colleague's region, which was now number three, and people started wondering if my numbers were right. While I was taken aback at the doubt regarding the turnaround, I was pleased to share the work we had done that was steering the ship in the right direction.

When I shared my approach to elevating my region by focusing on a place of self-reflection and purpose-driven leadership, most did not care for it. But in quiet offline conversations with me, they said, "We need more leaders like you who think differently." It was in that moment that I knew I was on to something that was important, not only for this organization, but for others.

Performance-Based Leadership—Short-Term Gains, Long-Term Failures

I was speaking with a senior leader when I asked, "Shouldn't we be speaking to our teams more about the five-year strategy so people see where they fit into the context of the organizational goals?" The senior leader said, "We have shared it, but let me worry about the strategy. I need people to focus on the current twelve-month results." Needless to say, I left that situation frustrated because it was a binary response. People will either hit a goal or not, and this can lead to elation or frustration. There is no in between. Had we taken people down a five-year journey, knowing that some years we might not hit the target but if people are attuned to the purpose we might actually achieve it, wouldn't that have given people a sense of accomplishment?

The cycle continued: some months were good, and energy was wasted when we were off course. That vicious cycle continued until, one by one, people left the organization, including myself and the leader with whom I had the conversation. The organization has moved on as it's difficult to bring down large organizations with individual leadership changes. However, think about the possibility of a purpose-driven organization and how much could have been accomplished had we focused on purpose over performance.

Turning Point Leadership—Focus on Purpose and Message Flow

In another situation, I was coaching a senior quality leader who wanted to improve results in complaint management. Technically, we could fix the process and get the desired result. However, when I asked the leader what they wanted to achieve, he said he wanted to spend more time with their customers in partnering relationships. There was no mention of complaint management, but a focus on a greater purpose and building relationships.

The turning point for this leader was understanding and teasing out their purpose. Think about the changes in messaging and the potential for a different set of solutions. In this case, the leader's messaging moved from "fixing" the complaint management process to "messaging" to leadership the need to build partnering relationships. The conversation moved from a set of actions for reducing complaints to one about how to get more closely aligned with customer expectations, now and in the future. Talk about a game changer in terms of this person's leadership and ability to drive a strategic plan!

This turning point of finding purpose in what you do is often a quick adjustment, but leaders don't often take the time to go through the exercise of defining it. We let the company ravage us with yearly performance results and we're chastised for not meeting them. Could your leadership be the first of many who stop to question what your purpose is? Only then can your team align to it.

Word of Caution on Purpose Before You Take the Leap

Purpose alone, without a sound foundation in the other compass points, will not give you peace of mind. Purpose is the glue that transcends every communication with your team and intimate one to one conversations (1-2-1s) with an employee. Purpose grounds the conversation when we're not on track. When we have purpose for the organization and ourselves, we give our employees something to anchor onto so they can align the work they do to the greater purpose. We bring their minds to work, not just their hands to perform a transaction.

Purpose is essential to starting the journey to peace of mind, but it's not the be-all and end-all. It's the framework of the ship, leveraging the points on the compass; it's what you pull on when the last few steps are to Peace of Mind. Purpose is a tool to rally the team, and is quite powerful, but is only successfully executed in concert with the other compass points.

What Does Lack of Purpose Look Like?

My engineering training teaches me to understand the symptoms of a problem before we can state the problem and go fix it. So, if we're aligned, let's take a deeper look into what it means to lack purpose. While I describe what I mean, take a moment and reflect on yourself and how you feel when there is a lack of purpose.

- You are unable to articulate *why* you are doing what you're doing.
- You are unable to align tactical work to strategic objectives, assuming strategic objectives exist.
- You are unable to communicate messages based on risk and impact to a greater cause.
- You lack confidence in your voice and others notice it.
- You lack the foundation to inspire others toward an outcome.
- The work you do is simply transactional for short-term results.

These are my prompts to get you to think about lack of purpose. If you've never thought about this because the purpose or vision of the organization has been cascaded down to you, then that's strike one against you. You've not taken the time to think. If the organization has not cascaded a purpose or vision and you continue to lead without creating one for yourself, strike two. If you've taken the time to reflect on your purpose and created the strategy to execute the purpose, but your team does not understand it, strike three. The purpose of what you do and how your leadership uses it to guide everything you do is critical to peace of mind and leveraging the collective alignment of your team.

Before sharing a story about the importance of purpose, it's time to pause and talk about you. I need you to review these questions, take out a pad of paper, go to your whiteboard or wherever you give yourself the space to bring forward your thoughts, and let them speak to you. If you don't have the time now, please put down the book. You need this time because it's critical to your leadership. When you do have time, pick this book up again and spend just five minutes thinking about your purpose—really think and see and feel what the work is that your leadership is meant to do. We'll return to my stories when you're done.

Your Time to Think About Purpose

- Do you have a personal purpose statement or an outcome you'd like to achieve?
- Is this purpose visible to you? Can you see it in your future, but are perhaps unclear on how to get there?
- If you see your purpose, do you have a support system or a roadmap to get there? Do you know who can help you, do you know whom to trust?
- Does your organization have a clearly stated purpose? If not, can you create one?
- What questions would you start to ask about the purpose (if it exists)? Would the team behave differently if they focused on purpose over performance?

Running on Empty/Racing to Find Purpose

In the last chapter, I shared how I was without peace of mind while leading an organization through chaos without having our work aligned on a singular purpose. My whiteboard was filled with pictures, words, and phrases with a few circles around clusters of related concepts. The purpose for why and how I was leading continued to evade me. Sometimes, as leaders, the answers cannot be found, but instead, they find us. I was patient but running on empty, and I had to find answers fast.

I really, really hate running, but that doesn't keep me from using it as a vehicle to rise above and overcome the challenge until I get into flow. Playing music while running lessens the physical challenge and eases both the body and mind into flow. It was in this place that the answers came to me—and then I cried. If you've never experienced a moment when logic and technical problem-solving has evaded you only for it to come to you out of the blue, you've never experienced insight. These "a-ha" moments don't come often, but when they do, they can be wrought with emotion, often called an epiphany.

I didn't want to work so hard. I didn't want my people to work so hard. I wanted for all of us to work less and spend more time doing the things we wanted to do, like being with family, friends, and community. I also wanted to build trust in the eyes of our customers and I wanted to be their favorite company to work with, not necessarily number one.

This purpose of what I wanted to achieve was swirling, and unrelated words on my whiteboard came to me in "The Framework of One." The Framework of One was about one team working in one way toward one goal. If I could create a framework of unity across the team and align all stakeholders on our purpose, then I could move the organization.

The purpose became quite clear to me—to be the favorite vendor of our customers while enabling our team to spend more time doing the things they love to do. This was based on a principle of building strong relationships that we could depend on; "number one" became meaningless. It was also about building a better framework for our associates so they didn't have to work so hard and could have energy for themselves as well as innovating at work instead of being slaves to the activity.

That picture came through to me so strong that I could see what it looked like. That became the centerpiece of my entire strategy; from there, we could build the pillars, the resources, the roadmaps, and the tangible goals we wanted to achieve. I was running because I was lost, but once I found my purpose, I raced at it and pulled my team over the finish line. But that will be for another chapter.

Turning Purpose into Action

Once you find your purpose and you can articulate it and translate it for the masses, I offer a few next steps for you if you've never been given the tools to translate purpose (strategy) into action (tactical). Before I share those tools, I want to pause and ask you a very important question. When has anyone ever shown you how to create purpose and align a strategy for it along with an action plan? Were you lucky enough to take a course in school to teach you this? Did you come up in your career as a subject matter expert and were you simply given a plan instead of thinking for yourself to create one?

Most CEOs have the ability to define purpose. But I ask for you to reflect on the people on your team. If they've never been asked to create their own purpose statement, then they will simply nod their heads in acknowledgement when you share yours. Unless you help them to translate purpose into their own strategy and tactical plans for their work, they will not fully understand the essence.

After we go through the tactical steps, I propose that you pause and reflect on whether your next level of leadership has these skills. It may be the most important workshop you conduct with them to build their understanding, give them new skills, and earn their trust.

Framework for Building a Strategy

- State the purpose
- Explain why it is important
- Establish the foundation or programs that are nonnegotiable and transcend all activity
- Explain the "how" with three key pillars (or more) that enable the strategy
- List the detailed work included in the pillars
- Identify the resources or teams that enable the work
- Create a high-level roadmap for all workstreams and interdependencies
- Create a roadmap for each functional area or workstream
- Create performance metrics and feedback loops for when you are off target
- Develop communication processes to align all efforts on collective progress toward the purpose
- Create a process for barrier removal/decision-making
- Have team members explain how their work aligns with the purpose

Don't Stop There—Ensure the Purpose is Aligned with Each Team Member

There's a specific reason why team members should explain how their work aligns with the purpose. I want you to pause on this one statement. When you arrive at a place of great clarity and the strategy makes complete sense to you, your work has only just begun.

While the team will fall into place and seek your direction on executing the plan, they will skip over aligning their purpose to yours and the organization's. When you take the time to ask the team to think about the strategy, develop their purpose, and seek connection to the work they are doing, you truly engage the employee in the greater outcome.

You do this thoughtfully, because you and only you know your team dynamics, but consider having everyone share their thoughts as a team. There is great value to having your team verbalize how they align to the purpose via the strategy. Some people will have great clarity while others will still not know what you're talking about. It's sad but true—I've seen this in the glassy eyes of my teams that don't get it at first. Some need to process this as in the past they've only been given marching orders and never the time to think and internalize their own purpose.

From there, the 1-2-1s you have with your employees should always start with the purpose of where you're going and how their work is aligned and performing against the greater outcome. Only then do we start from a place of creativity, greater perspective, and more intellectual conversations. Only once you've discussed the necessary strategic work should you go into the tactical work and barrier-removal conversations. I guarantee you the conversation will be more stimulating for both of you when you lead with your minds and strategic direction instead of starting with tactical work. Here's one example where one of my managers turned the corner in their work.

Moving an Organization from Activity-Based Performance Measurements to Purposeful work

One of my managers was beholden to an archaic performance measurement system of how many transactions they completed on behalf of our customers, based on volume and closure rates, by which metric my manager excelled globally; however, they were working themself into the ground.

While proud of their accomplishments, we discussed planning for the following year and how we could move the organization. This person immediately went to tactical proposals, including getting additional resources and aligning with other functional groups to take on their share of the work. Often, this person was so hyper-motivated to solve customer issues that they took on the work of others as the path of least resistance.

When I asked them about the current state of customer relationships and how they saw moving to a higher level of partnership in the coming year, they drew a blank. They reverted to complaining about the workload and how they did not have time to build more relationships with a greater pool of customers.

When I pressed again about where were they now in terms of the number of high-value relationships and where they would like that number to be, they said in addition to the four they had now, there really should be a total of ten to support growth of the business.

With that, the conversation went in a completely different direction with a well-defined purpose; from there, we build a roadmap across multiple workstreams that would enable the person to spend more time with customers and less in activity-based work. I'm pleased to say the frustration level of this highly effective professional decreased and the impact of the relationships increased in a way that enabled more business.

Essential Tools to Get Started with Building Strategies for Your Team

Bonus tools can be found at:
https://dropinceo.com/theceoscompass

- Purpose Statement Tool
- High-Level Roadmap Tool
- Crisis Scale—where are you in the spectrum of change and prioritization of your work

NOTE: These tools are not project management tools, of which there are many that exist for the individual who has oversight responsibilities. These are unique tools that I've created that have served me and may help you and your team to develop a purpose-driven strategy.

Are You Ready to Move On?

The CEO's compass is going to unfold now at a rapid rate, and I ask: are you truly ready? Have you given yourself a few hours to be in the moment while reading this content? If not, I propose you put the book down again until you are ready. Being in the moment is critical for a leader to receive insights and then to think about their own situation and be inspired to try new things. Not *my* things, but *your* things. It's a critical step in taking out the compass and starting your journey. If you are ready to start, let's continue to the next chapter.

*Sharing your past is important
so you can create meaningful
relationships in the future.*

CHAPTER 5

Compass Point: The Past, Skipping the Past is a Recipe for Failure

When we dig deep into a person's culture or past, we learn a lot about the individual. I have often found that organizations put teams together or integrate business units and fail at the most fundamental level of getting to know each other as people. We are missing data from the past that is critical to decision-making in the future. We fail to build trust and meaningful relationships. Without building trust, we miss the opportunity to advocate for change. When we see people simply as transactions, we don't fully honor who they are and what they contribute. I would compare this to the "culture," or those treasures that one brings forward into the current situation. Our people are all rich in information and yet we don't pause to understand it. While this compass point is meant for team dynamics, it is also in support of who you are to get you back on track.

Ask yourself what unique skills, experiences, personal values, and traits are special to you and no one else. What made you special to your parents, friends, classmates, teachers, community, and work that people have noted in you? It's important to remember these qualities that are the best parts of you.

Now think of those qualities you have that people have called out as different and which they thought were perhaps detrimental. I want you to acknowledge those as forgotten characteristics of who you are. This is your past and you cannot forget it. When we allow others to judge who we are, we lose the best parts of ourselves. We may not achieve our fullest potential. As a leader, it's important to recognize that in yourself. As a people leader, it is your duty to understand the past and the deep qualities of others that may not be known.

What Is Your Past? I'll Share Mine First to Get You Started

I was a very creative child who could sing, dance, write, draw, and speak extensively. Did I mention I could talk? If I haven't shared that with you yet, I could talk, A LOT! I could talk so much about what happened in my day, what I was processing out loud, and what I could see in the future that people asked me to be quiet. My parents listened to me as it brought them great joy, but the opposite was true in school.

My report cards each semester would acknowledge I was an extremely bright child, but that I tended to be a bit disruptive. Could my parents help them to keep me quiet? That was the beginning of a long period of time where the deep qualities of who I was were being squelched by society. As I entered the school system, conformity was the death of my creativity. I lost my creativity and gift of communication numerous times, and each time it started to be expressed again, it was not met with societal accolades.

So, turning back to you, think about those things that are at the core of who you are and that you don't bring forward into everyday life. Is there something from your past that is so special but you don't share it with others? Does it make you unique, but you don't want to stand out? Think about the same question in terms of your team. What do you not know about them? You better find out soon before it's too late. Here is another story about how to leverage the past and turn it into a WIN in the context of teams.

Success Story by Starting with the Past as Your Compass Point

We had one year to get a newly acquired company onto our ERP systems and bring them into our portfolio of offerings to our customers. The project team was assembled and led by IT, and project management resources were deployed. All the mechanics of a rapid transformation were in place that should have resulted in a precise execution that would prevent disruption of services to our customers. Although I count my piece of the project as a success, the sad truth was that the project failed at the enterprise level and brought the supply chain to a halt, infuriating our customers.

In my workstream that was focused on quality characteristics, I knew there were pieces missing and I raised various questions about resource capacity and capability, change management, and alignment with past customer requirements. All of these questions were politely acknowledged and put on a task list to be addressed—someday. Seeing that within my area of control, I needed to make my own assessment and identify gaps to address.

We deployed an independent team to create a purpose to embrace the historical cultures and come out as one unified organization. We spent considerable time with the individuals at the newly acquired site to understand their areas of expertise. We learned that with our acquisition, resources they had in the past no longer existed and we had to bridge that knowledge gap with resources in our own organization. We had to understand what made this company highly successful and leverage those characteristics in the new company. This meant understanding their customers' past expectations and making sure we accounted for that in the future. If something had to change, we made sure we worked with the customer to understand how their product or service would change. We also had to hire people because the acquisition resulted in some talent leaving the company. To go through an integration is challenging, and without sufficient resources, we would fail.

Fast forward—knowing their past culture, we developed a plan to assure that all change management gaps were addressed. We never disrupted the customers' quality as we went through the change and we maintained their loyalty. While the operations had challenges meeting service levels, there were few to no quality complaints. This happened because by engaging in this process of understanding the past, we built trust in the people we brought forward into the future. They were loyal and resourceful based on a common purpose and the fact that we respected them. We leveraged their past and talents and aligned them with the resources to make them successful.

When you have a common compass point on purpose and you acknowledge your people's pasts, achieving true north or peace of mind is assured.

Now it's Time for You to Think About the "Past" Compass Point

I think it's important to start with understanding your own past. When we start with you and the unique qualities of your personality, and why you do or do not bring them forward, then we can extend the exercise to your employees. Start with you, and at the end of the questions, change "you" to "your employees."

- What are the characteristics of who you are in every-day life that people acknowledge in a positive way?
- What are the characteristics you hide away because of how people have responded to them in the past?
- What are the characteristics of who you are that you never reveal to others?
- Why do you not share them?
- How would you feel if you could bring forward all of the characteristics of who you are from your past and now?
- Would your contribution to yourself, your team, your community, or career benefit from your past? In what way?
- **Go back to the beginning and ask the same questions about your employees.** Do you know their pasts and have you brought that forward?

It's Never Too Late to Start With the Past. Here's What You Can Do Now

You've been a leader of a team or an organization and you think it's embarrassing to go back in time to understand the past and the individual and collective culture of your team. I challenge you to think differently, as self and team discovery can be done at any time. Think of it as an "evolution" instead of simply an initiative or back-tracking to something you could have done in the past. Your team will appreciate it, and through the process, you will grow trust with your team.

Actions you can do now

- Ask each team member to share details about their personal, educational, community, and career journey.
- Start collecting unique qualities from each that were not known before so you have an inventory of the gifts they bring to the team.
- As team members share similar characteristics, group them together and take account of how often they have a shared past. This becomes part of the future culture and values system.
- Celebrate the differences and unique characteristics people have. Their gift from the past may be a necessary tool in the future.
- After taking inventory of the common characteristics of the past, ask each member to share a value they would like to see as part of their future and collectively vote for 1-2 additional characteristics.

- Create a blended set of characteristics and values that leverages the past and the future to start to create a culture of the future.

My Past Compass Points to Inspire You to Think About Yours

My journey to create the CEO's compass is rooted in my personal experiences, some of which I've shared in previous chapters. Here is my journey into the past compass point.

I was floored by and grateful for the immense talent that I had built up around me as I forged ahead with my new quality organization. One manager had deep relationships with some critical customers from past roles that we needed to maintain. Another manager had a passion for history and educating others, but they had been buried in transactional work before I brought them into my continuous improvement function. One leader of the organization was a certified auditor whose skill could be leveraged to benefit my other plants as well as their home plant. My latest hire had worked for one of our customers and was critical to navigating quality challenges by leveraging that preexisting trust.

Having taken inventory of my organization, I was able to place the individuals in the right functions for their talents. They were smarter than me, and I needed to know everything about what they did, who they knew, and what they were good at to accelerate a challenging transformation of the quality organization. As I assembled the talent into their functional areas of expertise and contribution, the strategy unfolded in support of our purpose. The purpose unfolded in concert with the past, into:

Embrace the Past and Come Out as One

This spawned the framework of one—one team, working in one way, toward one goal. I shared this in our compass point chapter titled "Purpose."

Let my story inspire you to think about how you'll discover the past. The CEO's compass places past and purpose very close to each other to remind you that together, they can get you back on track to peace of mind.

Take a breath. Put down the book. Think about how you'll discover the past—yours and that of your team. It's a compass point many leaders do not pause to consider. You can be the leader that your team needs; you can create a lasting impact by the trust and relationships you'll grow. When you're ready, pick up the book and let's continue.

Recognizing talent and bringing it forward is the greatest gift we can give humanity.

CHAPTER 6

Compass Point: Pride, The Intersection of Humanity and Intellectual Property

Pride is a special compass point because I don't often see it spoken about in the context of team dynamics. We often speak of it in emotional terms, but it's also a unique characteristic of an individual or organization. Pride is the intersection of the human and intellectual property. When we bring teams together, we know they comprise subject matter experts, but we fall short of understanding the sum total of the individual accomplishments that have brought them to this point in time.

Pride is also a business issue, and if you do not see it as a significant compass point, it can have a negative outcome. We waste time, money, and effort solving problems when the information lies within. We create lack of trust among team members when we don't care to ask them for their input or insight. This often manifests itself in getting blindsided because we're too focused on quick results. Ultimately, when we skip over pride and asking people what they think or know, we lose intellectual property.

What for many years was celebrated as craftmanship has recently been boiled down to commodities. People are simply a number; if you lose one, you go out and hire another. This cycle continues to erode our business until it's too late and we've lost our competitive advantage. That's why it's so important to not only acknowledge the pride of individuals but also preserve the legacy by capturing the intellectual property in terms of training. I use the term "intellectual property" to describe an individual's valuable knowledge and experience to elevate this component and recognize that there is a business risk if we don't take inventory of it. When we instead speak in terms of "subject matter expertise," we minimize the risk of losing these resources. The only time we feel the impact of losing our intellectual property is when we lose market share. When we lose human intellectual property, our brand starts to decay. When we value our employees pride and expand the intellectual property through training and mentoring programs, we reduce this risk to our organization.

When we arrive at today, we find that we may have the skills to do a task but are not asked to share our skills, nor what else we can do.

We only think in terms of the here and now, and fall short of recognizing the collective potential of an individual or a team to create a certain outcome. We speak about that in Chapter 4, "Purpose." I know I've made mistakes around recognizing pride, which is why I now bring it forward as a key compass point.

Can You See Pride in Your Organization?

I'll never forget this one process improvement activity at a flavor manufacturing plant to reduce quality defects associated with operator error. We had many experienced senior operators; the errors were coming from new hires. We realized we needed to capture the experience of the senior operators in order to preserve their intellectual property as they retired. I was paired up with the trainer in an effort to systematically capture their knowledge into standard operating procedures. What I experienced in that process ignited my journey to see human-centric leadership.

The person was kind, generous, and an utmost professional: clearly a leader within the operator ranks. He was delighted to share what he knew as well as why it was important. He carefully laid out every step in their process, and I became quite emotional about it. The closest human to the products, second only to the consumers, showed how much they cared about quality and was proud of their knowledge. They were proud to train others in what they knew. They were clearly leaving a lasting impact because their pride showed in everything they said and did.

I miss that person because they taught me an important lesson in pride. Pride is personal and reflects how you take great care in what you do. It is even more noble to share your intellectual property with others without reservation. Most people have a sense of pride, but if we don't show we care, they bury it never to be seen again. In the race to get results, we can lose the human, and if we lose them, we lose their minds. We default to a transaction.

I share this story for you to think about a time when you experienced great pride and were recognized for it. I share this with you to ask if you have seen someone with great pride and their joy of being acknowledged. Pause to reflect about how you felt, and ask yourself, is this something that is missing in your life or in the lives of the teams you lead?

The Pitfall of Ignoring Pride in Leadership

I was leading a process improvement team to improve equipment yields in the flavor industry. We sent the engineers to make process adjustments and later found that the operators had undone the adjustments that we'd made. When we asked the operators why they switched back, they said they got better yields with the old adjustments. We made the changes again and the operators switched them back again.

I thought the operators were simply being difficult until I realized we'd made a critical mistake. We failed to bring them into the planning meetings for the changes. When we finally did invite them to those discussions, we found a wealth of previously untapped knowledge. We discussed the desired outcome as a team and collectively agreed on the necessary adjustments. Needless to say, we got better results and the project moved forward.

I'm embarrassed to say as a trained Lean and Six Sigma Blackbelt continuous improvement professional, I failed in the area of change management. Change management concerns bringing in all affected parties to explain the changes and get buy-in. That's a check in the box to say you did it, but the missing element was approaching it from a place of pride.

Where I failed was in rushing to check the box and stay on track with the project. I missed the human dimension of the project. I missed digging deep into the knowledge of 20–30-year employees. If we're lucky they teach you this in your

Continuous Improvement certifications, but I'm afraid most do not. They teach you how to technically manage projects, not how to manage humans and their intellectual property. That is why pride is critical to the CEO's compass.

So, I ask you this:

- How have you felt when you were told to "keep your head down" and simply do the task that was required?
- How would you feel if someone took the time to acknowledge your pride/gifts and pull them forward?
- Have you ever asked the people on your team about what are they most proud of in the work they do and the intellectual property they have known or not known?
- What would it look like if you brought this out from all your team members? Would it bring a whole new dimension to the way they work?

Turning the Ship with Pride

When we take the time to understand the past (culture) and pride (human and intellectual property), we build trust. If you tell people that you care about them as people, they will give you much more than you ask for. When you only focus on people, process, and platforms, you may get short-term results but fail to sustain those gains. As you look at the CEO's compass, you will see that pride is next to performance. These two compass points, used together, leveraging pride, will get you the performance results you desire. People are incredible when you gain their trust; they will give you 200 percent of what they know and what they can give. People will be resourceful and work hard because they'll use their intellectual property to find a solution.

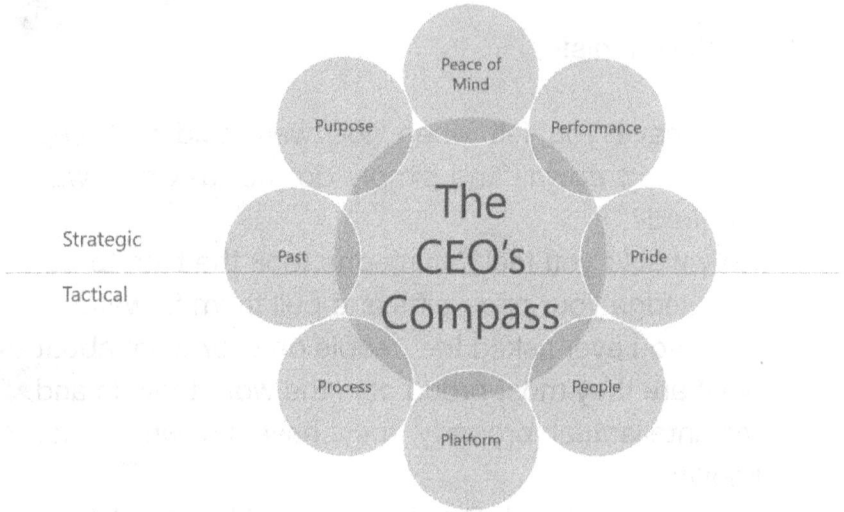

What Can You Do Now to Leverage the Power of Pride?

I've learned that a few simple tools you can use right now are enough to give you insight into the pride of your team and how best to leverage them to improve performance, leading you to peace of mind.

- Meet with each individual and create a SWOT analysis (Strengths, Weaknesses, Opportunities, Threats).
- Merge the data together to get a high-level view of your entire team.

- Create work standards from people with similar strengths to sustain your intellectual property.
- Where people have an aligned strength and weakness, pair them together to learn from each other and build capability.
- Ask the people with strengths in certain subjects to share with others so everyone can benefit.
- Where there are opportunities, plan how you will leverage or build capability in the team.
- Immediately mitigate threats that can deteriorate pride in the team.

This is nothing more than building a high-performance team, leveraging pride as a compass point to get you back on track.

Where Pride Came Together on My Journey

I had inherited talent from an acquisition and had them placed on plant-specific improvement teams. I knew they had tremendous customer and product knowledge, but in the moment I could not leverage that expertise. Then we got a customer complaint, and here is how leveraging pride paid off.

When we started to ship product from a new plant to a customer, the labels and documentation were not correct. I knew this person had experience with this customer and products, so I immediately deployed them to the customer to work on the problem. Given that this person knew what the customer had expected in the past, they quickly moved in to provide assurance that they would take care of the issue. They used their past knowledge and were quickly able to correct the issue and get back on track. I was able to observe the problem resolve itself and provide leadership to the person who was taking care of the issue.

Had I not taken the time to get to know this person's area of expertise and unique intellectual property, the impact to the customer relationship could have been devasting. I realize for some, this may seem obvious. However, have you ever seen the leader who jumps in to put the fire out themselves? They cause more damage in the process, even if only to themselves and others in the form of stress and chaotic activity. When we know the talent on our team and provide them the opporutnities to leverage their pride, the results are faster and have greater impact.

This is the reason why in all my interactions and networking, I start with asking the person: "Tell me about yourself. What are you passionate about, what was your career journey, and how did you arrive at the work you're doing now?" Try this out and you'll gain so much insight into their pride. You never know when you'll need to use this compass point to get you back on track!

Before moving onto the next part of the CEO's compass, take a moment to remember what you've internalized from the previous points. This is important, because we've discussed topics that are highly emotional and personal. We don't want to forget how we felt and what we want to start doing tomorrow. Peace of mind, purpose, pride, and past were the missing pieces to my leadership journey.

As we move into people, process, platform, and performance, I want to set an expectation. These are NOT what you think. I will present a completely different view on how to think about these compass points. If I were to regurgitate what we already know about these compass points, you could put the book down now as having no further value. What I propose to you is that you open your mind to a new perspective as we take you on this journey—your journey.

If you're ready, turn the page!

"Success as a leader requires effort. Get to know your team as people first, understand their potential as professionals, trust and empower them to get the job done."

—*Germain St-Denis, The Architect of People First.*

CHAPTER 7

Compass Point: People, People are the Greatest Tool in Your Toolbox

I often wonder why all people can't be high performers. Society forces us to put people on a bell-shaped curve and judge them along a line from poor performers, to Steady Eddies, to high performers. We are forced to profile people based on performance measurements that are based purely on results and impact to the business. While there are tools such as the "9-box" that also grade people on potential, they fall short of creating an action plan to enable everyone to be a high performer.

For the poor performer, we simply accept them for how they show up; if it's too hard to improve them, we pass them off and eventually they leave or are asked to leave. If they're a Steady Eddie, they show up, do their work, and we pay them a passing compliment. We depend on them to be loyal and do the work as needed. If they don't speak up and show initiative, we leave them there and don't invest our time in improving them. We believe they'll always be there for us — until one day, uninspired to stay, they move on. For the high performers, we are proud to have them on our team. We applaud them and actively seek ways to mentor and groom them for the next role. We get excited about them and we develop action plans to develop the next level of leadership or impact.

But back to my original question: why can't all people be high performers? We hire people into the organization with high expectations, and we invest in resources needed to run the business. Thus, I ask you another question: when you see that someone is not a high performer, do you take the time to ask why? Do you spend time meeting with them, setting clear expectations, and providing feedback in the context of what to continue, start, or change? Why do people start to fall into these profiles of high, medium, and low performance? Have you noticed how by not Investing in people, they become an expense to the bottom line?

I am a proponent of the idea that every employee is responsible for their own performance and personal development. A highly aware individual must take that accountability and align with their boss and stakeholders to ensure they're on track. If not, they should solicit feedback on what to continue, start, or change.

But let's talk about you and the role you play. What do you see as your role in not only investing in the people but ensuring they all have the ability to be high performers? Do you meet with them regularly and align their work with the greater Purpose? Do you discuss their development opportunities with them—do you even know how to provide feedback? I know I'm asking you a lot of questions, but this chapter is meant to make you think instead of doing what you have done in the past. It is meant to open your mind up to the idea that everyone can be a high performer and to make you consider what your role is in ensuring that.

The impact of not addressing the "people" compass point can be devastating, and it will require a lot of energy and time to get back to peace of mind. It is on the far side of the compass, and if this is where you have problems, it can pull you way off course.

If you're not sure that this problem exists, you can see it manifest in the following ways.

- There are individual performance issues that people talk about and which maybe you've not noticed yet or have ignored.
- People focus on activity-based work and do not see the strategic alignment and greater purpose of their work. They stress over the work; they miss meetings or opportunities to mingle outside of work. They become invisible.
- People start to lose their confidence, they stop speaking up, their eyes are down or they are aloof.
- Your people are ineffective at communications, unable to process feedback, and have limiting beliefs in what they are capable of.
- People operating as poor performers become an expense to the organization.
- You lose top-line growth because you don't ask for people to think and bring new ideas. The Steady Eddies will keep their heads down and do the work. They won't think and bring the best they have to serve you.

The Turning Point: When Leaders Become Mentors

The turning point came to me long after I had invested in my people, when I was questioned by executive leadership on my dream team. They questioned why I had such a large team and if I really needed them all. They started to question my numbers because we improved our quality metrics so quickly. The secret was not the technical expertise or volume of work they could do, but the quality of the work did have a direct impact on the outcome of the strategy we built. I was building a team of high performers—every one of them! During my journey to turn around the performance of my region, I had pulled together a team of subject-matter experts from all areas whom I needed to help achieve my strategy.

My team had been labeled in the past as simple subject-matter experts, and many outside of my team didn't quite understand how my people were going to be the key to getting us out from being the last in my region. My team members had not been seen as leaders and had been labeled as difficult to deal with and not promotion material. And you know, these doubters would have been right—had they been in charge of my team. My colleagues were traditional leaders who saw the role of sponsor as simply someone to be reported to and to troubleshoot when performance results were not achieved. It is a wasteful dynamic to which minor improvements can be made, but which lacks depth for building sustainable results.

I, however, saw the talent in each one of these individuals. They had their unique qualities (past) and expertise far greater than mine (pride), and I saw great untapped talent that needed to be brought forward for greater impact. I took the time to understand their individual pain points and performance challenges. I took the time to understand their limiting mind-sets. I took the time to see where their talent was wasted and should have been applied to a different role. Rarely do leaders spend this amount of time to understand their people. It takes a lot of time, but as I said earlier, the investment in people is critical before it becomes an expense.

Often, as in this example, the investment pays off. When the results came in, we had moved from last place to the second position out of four regions. The results came quickly from hard work on all of our parts, but also because of the mentoring I provided to each individual, encouraging them to try new things and create a greater impact by how they showed up and what technical expertise they provided.

One leader was exceptional in compliance, but was frustrated when people did not always listen. When we gave him feedback suggesting he position information in the context of risk and impact—and also that he should stand while delivering information—his messages were amplified and people listened.

Another leader was activity-based and had no experience in creating a long-term plan to change the impact of what they were doing. As soon as we identified the gaps in their roadmap, we were able to project their technical expertise into proactive, meaningful work that ultimately built more customer loyalty and partnerships.

Finally, one employee was a subject matter expert in projects, but they were a rock star at influencing change in continuous improvement. This was a skill that was needed to move people from simply fixing issues to permanently removing the root causes. This person shined when they were an educator, and we could see we needed to shift their role. When we moved them into the new role, they had renewed energy and were able to solve some very significant issues. This rock star later left the company only to become a leader in another organization and have a greater impact. I'm grateful for knowing them, and knowing that an investment in people enabled them to become a high performer.

I was fortunate to already have talented people on my team, but I took the time to not simply be their sponsor and leader, but their mentor. I ask of you now: do you have time to take on a new mentorship role for your people? If not yourself, how can you construct a program that builds people so they're all rock stars?

This Makes Sense, but Where Do You Start?

It starts with you. Please do not pass this off to someone else to do. Instead, seek a partner who can go through the process with you. This book will give you techniques that have worked well to build up my team of individuals. As we move into the next chapter (on process), we'll further expand its application to the team, and later, the platform, or the tools they need for high performance. While this may resemble building "high-performance teams," it's more about how it's integrated into your compass. You see, if you only work on people, it may start to bring you back on track, but you have to look at it in relationship to the other compass points because changes in one direction may impact others.

For example, if you only work on building up people's essential skills but fail to align those with purpose, you only move the needle slightly in one direction. This and subsequent chapters are meant to help you think about how addressing people's performance in alignment with other compass points will pull you toward peace of mind. When people are supported in building their skills by intentional mentoring and alignment to a well-defined purpose, getting to peace of mind is easy. When we mentor our people and take the time to also understand their past and pride, we build tremendous trust. People will follow us and support us through all situations or crises.

What I have found in other books are operating systems designed to elevate organizational performance and impact presented in a detailed step-by-step approach. In a perfect world, following a five-step process would work. When you introduce variables such as service issues, recalls, changes in leadership, acquisitions—the list can go on forever—then operating systems fall short of having a lasting impact. We fail to understand the interaction between the environment and the system. While we can create risk assessments and mitigation plans to avert crises, the truth of the matter is, it doesn't speak to how people are your greatest tool to defeat these complex situations. Well-supported individuals, and I mean ALL individuals on your team, will work with you to get back on track.

When we leverage the compass, we can get back on track faster than we would by throwing out the old system, bringing in new leadership, or throwing good money after bad. Remember when we started this book? We said you were a rock star until situations changed you and you lost your confidence. You had lost your way. When it comes to people, the support you give them is probably your best investment in the business. These steps are the foundation of my human-centric leadership curriculum and the difference between a high performer and someone who once was or who aspires to be one.

Mindset—Don't Take it for Granted

Mindset is the belief of what you can and cannot do and is often described as "open" or "closed." People with an open mindset think in terms of what *is* possible vs. what *is not* possible. Through self-awareness and an inventory of your own mindset, we can proceed to unpack what is/is not working for you. Starting with your mindset will enable the rest of the work we do together. I suggest we discuss this in the context of yourself before you can see the power of how it can be used as a tool to mentor your team. When we develop the skill to be aware of our mindset and make changes that serve us, we can then help others.

There are three reasons why mindset is important in developing yourself and ultimately your employees.

- When you have a limiting belief about yourself, you project that to the world and they see you the same way, which influences the opportunities they offer you.
- When you have a positive mindset that is not fully projected, it's important to understand what holds you back.
- When you have the right mindset but the environment you are in does not support it, we need to think of ways to position you for success.

The reason we struggle with this is that people will judge the results they get based on the interactions they have with their environment. This is called situational data. They never take inventory of their own qualities, and without doing so, they cannot take accountability for the results. This is called reflective data. We always focus on what is clearly in front of us, such as situational data, and don't take the time to reflect on our view of ourselves and our relationships past, present, and future. It's this reflective data we often skip that is critical for self-discovery before moving forward.

In order to overcome this, you need to take inventory about how you feel about your current state. Write down what you are proud of and do well. What are you frustrated about that is not getting the right result? Do you show up the same in all places or do you present yourself differently in different environments? What parts of you do you not show? What are your fears? What do you believe about who you are? What do you love? What do you wish you could do more of? What holds you back? What do you hide from others? Do you feel like you could accomplish so much more? Are there people around you who believe in you or who believe that you could do more? Are you your own advocate or do you seek approval from others?

What activities do you do that bring you to a place of calm and clear thinking (walking, listening to music, day dreaming, exercise)?

Unpack your mindset: being comfortable with the uncomfortable!

If you've never unpacked mindset because it's an uncomfortable place to start a conversation, I sincerely ask that you get over this discomfort. If you can't unpack this, someone else will. It's a bit harsh to say that, but I've had numerous people unpack their mindset with me as part of a mentoring relationship. I think to myself, how many bosses out there are missing the full potential of their employees because they're speaking to me and not them? If you need help unpacking their mindsets, seek the support of an expert, sometimes your HR business partner. DO NOT send them to an external course and expect them to be fixed. Do it from within and show them you care!

Confidence Is a Killer, Especially When You're a High Performer

One mentee said to me: "If I could only regain my confidence, the rest would be easy!" Their story was that they were once a high performer, but when they switched jobs, the environment was different and the same capabilities did not yield the same results. They lacked the skills to navigate and understand the differences, and along the way, they lost their confidence. During my time with them, I could see them as a higher performer, and during our time together, they regained their confidence and started to live up to that expectation. I did nothing with their technical capabilities, but instead unleashed potential by changing a mindset that did not serve them.

A Quick Exercise to Unpack Mindset

Here's a quick exercise to try on yourself to help you to mentor others. Identify the positive mindsets you have that impact the results you want to achieve. Anything that starts with "I am," "I can," "I will" is a mindset that serves you. Write down that positive belief and the characteristics of the environment that support that belief.

Now identify the negative mindsets that impact the results you want to achieve. Anything that starts with "I'm not," "I won't," "I can't," "I don't think" is a mindset that needs a deeper dive to understand how you gained it and what it has impacted. What are your negative beliefs and the characteristics of the environment that support those beliefs?

Once you are done with this exercise, you need to post these on a wall and simply acknowledge them. They are valid and they are who you are now. You need to own them before you can move on.

Now here's the test: start to listen to the words you say and those others say. Do you notice phrases such as "I'm not" and "I can't" showing up more often than you were previously aware they did? Look at the people who use these words and ask yourself, are they really "not" or do they simply have a limiting mindset? You'd be surprised how often people use these phrases and how infrequently we as leaders take the time to weed out this behavior.

Next time someone uses a negative mindset phrase, stop and ask them "why do you believe that?" You'd be surprised at how off-guard this will catch them. You may find that a couple minutes to pause and halt such a mindset is the best few-minutes' investment that you make all day!

Tears Are Important, Don't Shy Away from Them

While I was mentoring someone who was a talented and highly aware individual, early in our journey they choked up in tears. They realized that the only thing holding them back in their career was themself. They had strong limiting beliefs about their intelligence because of a legacy of family members who had not pursued higher education. They carried that belief and knew it was wrong, but owned it until the moment they shared it with me. I asked them to think about it, and they immediately knew it was holding them back. We later moved rapidly through our materials and now they're being considered for higher roles in the organization. It all started by considering their limiting mindset. So why can't you ask the same of yourself or your team? If you don't, you'll never achieve your full human potential.

Limiting beliefs are the tangible manifestations of a negative mindset that give you something you can start to work on with a person. When we start to ask questions about "why" we have these limiting beliefs, we get to the root cause of what perpetuates them and we can start to identify new behaviors to practice so we can move past them. We need to understand when these limiting beliefs started to exist and have an impact on who we are; very often, we developed them over time. Often, a limiting belief can originate from a specific event or be instilled by a single person. If the event or person no longer exists, it's important to stop owning it; it is also important to understand the event or situation to move past it. Finally, understanding how we project these limiting beliefs and how the world responds to them is important. As you practice new behaviors and the world reacts differently, you will know you're on a path to make the changes you desire.

The reason why this topic is difficult is that we don't often seek to understand how a person has arrived at their current state, stuck in their mindset. They sometimes don't take the time to articulate what is needed so they can put a "face" to it and then make the decision to do something about it. They claim a label and never seek to move beyond it.

To solve this issue, we need to acknowledge a limiting belief and how you arrived at it. Next, write down that limiting belief, and then write down what a positive belief looks like. Once you see the current state and future state, write down one action you can take to move you closer to the positive belief. Through this process, you are taking action.

I have you start this exercise with yourself because going through the process yourself helps you to see similar opportunities in your team and gives you the ability to unleash their potential.

Real-Life Example of Moving from a Limiting to a Positive Belief

My friend was interviewing for a job in technical sales but was not confident she would get the position because she'd never been in sales. The sales role would be for serving professionals just like herself, but she had a negative mindset—at least one of doubt. I told her she would be perfect for sales because she understood the technical challenges of the profession. She could speak the language of her customers and help them through their issues. After she gave this some thought, the narrative in her mind began to shift from "I can't" to "I can." That subtle shift in mindset enabled her to get the role and also a promotion in a short timeframe. While I can't take credit for her accomplishment, it is interesting how a spin on what you "can't" do becomes what you "can" do. Do you have an example within yourself where you shifted your limiting belief and got a positive result? Did you ever share that with your team as a way to inspire them?

When Opportunities Stall Due to Risk Paralysis

When we are aware of our beliefs both old and newly developing, we sometimes still feel helpless to make a change. We need to examine any barriers real or perceived and start to break them down. It's the difference between feeling helpless to change and having the power to make the changes.

Everything ultimately is in your control. It's simply a matter of identifying the right opportunity and the choices you have. With new mindsets and beliefs, we have to take action on these choices or practice them to validate how they can serve you. Sometimes we can't see the choices or how to manifest them and simply need some guidance on how to move from aspiration into action.

People will struggle because they get excited about the possibilities of shifting their mindset and simply don't know where to start. Excitement met with uncharted waters can leave them helpless. If they don't see how, they can guide the ship, they will sink at this point into deeper helplessness.

When we arrive at a place that we want to make conscious decisions about improving our performance as a goal, we want to leverage a strength and do more or maybe stop a behavior. We find we are held back or at a loss for how to move forward. It's important to document the items we want to start/stop/continue and then write down opportunities and choices. When we can write this down and express it, we can (a) discuss whether we see the full opportunity, (b) determine if it helps us reach our goals, (c) list the choices we have, (d) identify what holds us back, (e) decide on a direction, and (f) take an action. It sounds simple, but given the opportunity to think about it, most people draw a blank and don't know how to get started.

Start now with the mindset that everything is in your control. It's time to turn the actions into results. Identify the most important action you need take to help you move forward. Identify what will happen if you take this action. Identify what will happen if you do not take this action. Finally, write down how this action will get you closer to your ultimate performance goal.

You will find that by breaking down an action into smaller pieces, it reduces the anxiety that comes with risk-taking. People will be moved to action rather than being paralyzed by risk.

Take a Risk on Yourself; You Might Actually Be Successful

"Deb, you could be a plant manager or the CEO of a company." As usual, I looked at my husband and rolled my eyes and said, "No, I could never do that!" And now here I am a few years later, founder of Illumination Partners and running all aspects of a business. Why didn't I think I could do that? It was because I'd never "done that" and I didn't think I had the right technical capabilities. But when faced with the choice of going back to the job market after being let go, I knew the risk of not starting my business was greater to me personally than to move forward. Sometimes we're forced to take a chance on ourselves, but with this short story comes great insight. What if we posed this question to ourselves when faced with a challenge: "What if I'm successful?"

I heard this from a personal trainer I worked with many years ago and understood it, but never internalized it to the fullest. I remember preparing for a presentation and getting all nervous about it when he said "what if you're successful," and it changed my entire perspective. I'll never forget that great insight from a person passing through my life. I propose you ask "what if I'm successful" when you're faced with a risk, and pass that on to the people you lead. Think about the life-changing impact you may have on others!

When Good Intentions Stop Because We Lack Accountability Tools

We now have a positive mindset; we've unpacked our limiting beliefs, and we've confirmed a commitment to taking action. Then it all collapses because we've not equipped our people with the tools to keep them accountable. This parallels our commitment to lose weight or start a new hobby and then chastising ourselves for failing. I propose it's because we've not prepared ourselves and our people with the right accountability tools.

The solution to this is similar to the ways people learn. Some people learn by reading, others by listening, others by observing, and still others by physically doing. The same goes for commitment to change and the accountability support needed. The approach described below is simply a guide for you to find a way to be accountable. Pick a path that suits your style and try it out. If it doesn't work, nothing lost—simply experiment with another tool.

For me, I have an Excel spreadsheet as an accountability tool that shows my commitment to outcomes on a yearly, monthly, weekly, and daily timeframe. Each day I take an action, and by the end of the week, month, or year, I've achieved 80+ percent of what I set out to do. Without such incremental support tools, the daunting task of taking a risk or trying something new is exactly that: daunting.

But don't take my word for it—every mentee of mine who has used some form of an accountability tool for the changes they wanted to make has either been promoted, started an MBA, or quit their job in pursuit of more purposeful work.

So Much to Consume, But How to Do It on My Own?

Because I care so much about human-centric leadership and unleashing people's potential, I want to share with you these gifts. Everything in this chapter along with the accountability tool that has enabled me to achieve every milestone in my strategy is available to you.

These tools are available at:
https://dropinceo.com/theceoscompass

CHAPTER 8

Compass Point: Process, The Fairy-Tale—PDCA & DMAIC Don't Fix a Process

Traditional thinking around fixing the process is often to create a procedure or a flowchart, install a piece of equipment, or create a new user interface to improve experience, results, or performance. It's something often tangible that you can see the impact of in terms of results—quality, cost, experience, profitability. When we improve processes but then over time fail to produce results, we implement improvement teams, we put pressure on people, and we waste a lot of time and money. I've seen this pattern repeat itself over and over again, and then a new leader is installed in the hope that the process will improve. Where this goes awry is that it's a linear way of thinking. In the quality world, we implement Plan-Do-Check-Act (PDCA), or for more complex problems, we Define-Measure-Analyze-Improve-Control (DMAIC) and expect more significant results. What is missing from this linear way of improving processes is the human dimension. It is missing the human interactions with the process as well as the human-to-human interactions that will derail a process or make it less sustainable.

Don't get me wrong, these are magnificent methodologies that to this day I employ when I work with clients. They'll get the results you desire, but will you achieve the outcome or purpose of what the process is meant to deliver in a sustainable way? I've seen CEOs time and time again scratch their heads and wonder what went wrong. It bewilders them as they sit back and observe the process or, in the face of crisis, play referee to get it back on track. We fix the problem and live to see another day and claim success. However, when the problem rears its ugly head again, we have to question if we fixed the process. More importantly, did we fix the right process?

On the CEO's compass, "process" is defined as the interface of the individuals with the team. I propose it's the ability of the individuals to understand the strengths, weakness, opportunities, and threats (SWOT) that can close gaps and seek optimal performance. It's the ability to communicate difficult messages or give and receive feedback in order to make course corrections. All of these are skills that are critical for the interaction between individuals.

In general, managers do not enable the development of these skills in the people they lead, which is why they remain managers instead of leaders. Instead, they see the employee as a poor performer, and where they identify a critical deficiency, they send the employee to training. They then fail the individual by not reinforcing what was learned in this training and showing how to apply it to the current state. Even more troubling is the indirect impact on the customers when employees don't have these important skills. The employee and the lack of leadership become a risk to the business and potentially a financial liability. Where it's less critical, such managers often ignore the problem and hope it will go away. This then leads to deteriorating team dynamics, and then you have a crisis. Let's not forget the Steady Eddies on the team who do the work, but who in the face of crisis will only do what is expected of them and no more.

If you see underdeveloped skills, you know the business has failed to address the human process of problem solving and collaboration. Talent and creativity have been relegated to fixing issues over and over again, and the business fails to improve its performance. We send people into battle each day with a popsicle stick and a fly swatter when then they need a sword and a shield. Why do we do this? Do we not see that the process of people's interactions is critical to success?

Learning the Hard Way—Until It's Too Late

I had to fire my quality engineer because they were not delivering results and the way they worked was frustrating other people. The day I fired the person, they said to me "Just tell me what you need me to do and I'll do it" with their arms raised, looking helpless. The damage was done. I'd hurt my reputation by not seeing the problem and how to address it. I hurt the person because I had no process to hold courageous conversations or a framework to provide feedback. While they left the company, I had a sinking feeling in my heart; the worst was yet to come when I was eventually asked to leave the company myself.

I was a high performer, and I had the ability to build an organization in a startup; on the horizon was the possibility of an IPO and cashing in my stock options. As I was making these small mistakes in my leadership, I was making them alone. There was no person meeting with me on a monthly basis to provide feedback and give me the essential skills to better manage my people. They never replaced me after my departure, and after a small rise to glory, the company ultimately closed as the industry went bust.

I share this story with you as I wonder about the process of people development and providing the skills needed to be successful. I would think my boss would have seen where the dynamics were not working and helped to develop me so I could develop others. I learned a hard lesson with this story, and I have helped to develop a career development plan for every employee since who has come into my charge, as well as coach team dynamics as a greater purpose in my leadership roles.

So, I come back to you and ask whether you know or see what is missing in the team dynamics that will derail their short-term impact or long-term sustainability. Let me share what this looks like, and see if it resonates with you.

The Secret to Improving Team Dynamics for Sustainable Success

When helping a senior leader solve productivity and service issues in their operations, we found the problem was lack of leadership presence, not setting work standards for the team, and not having visible accountability for performance.

Spending money to further increase performance after you've addressed team effectiveness is money well spent. Spending money on the process shows that you trust how the team is performing and you want to support their future.

When leaders mentor the collective team dynamics, they leave a lasting legacy by giving people the tools to perform at a higher level.

This is something that many leaders overlook in favor of simply "fixing the process" when in fact it is the people processes that need to be strengthened. Leaders/sponsors of teams become much more accountable for the team's results when they actively engage in team performance and the essential skills they need.

I have dozens of tools that enable team dynamics, but I've picked some of the most impactful tools for you to implement immediately. You have the skills yourself in most cases, and now is your time to teach others. However, if you lack the skills because you have risen without having had the mentorship to develop these skills, this guide will help you.

Teach Your People to Think

Fix it now and fix it again tomorrow—your customers will become weary and leave the at the first chance they have to find a new supplier. Trust your people to find the root cause and your customers will remain loyal for a lifetime. Isn't that time and trust well spent?

When there is a problem, your people need to be able to first articulate a problem statement. Without that, the information they bring to you is noise without logical thinking. A tried and true tool to help evolve their problem statement is the "5W1H" approach (Who, What, Where, When, Why, and How Often). Now I will say that including a "Why" in the problem statement presumes they've found the root cause. However, a few preconditions will at least start a conversation. An example of a quality issue positioned this way could be: "The third-shift quality technician recorded an out-of-tolerance result for the product due to the density being out of spec; this trend has been increasing for the last three months for a total of five rejections."

What this means for the individual is that they had to think about the most critical information to bring to you to provide context and start a constructive dialog. The next step in the process is for them to propose a solution or call to action. The next sentence could be: "Due to this increasing trend over the past three months, I propose we get the team together (including R&D) and break down the possible causes of the issue before we impact service to our customers." In this sentence, not only have they proposed a next step, but they've also qualified the risk and impact.

Following this methodology of stating the problem, creating a proposal, and identifying risk and impact elevates the importance of your people and gives them the skills to think for themselves. This methodology can also be used when they are making presentations to other stakeholders to immediately elevate their thought leadership and spawn engaging conversation instead of simply a "report out."

Practice this on yourself to ensure you have the skills and then start sharing this with your team.

Position People for Their Strengths and Passion; You'll Get a Better Result

The disruptive person in the room is the leader whom businesses have not learned how to support. They leave and become the greatest entrepreneur while businesses miss out on innovation and creativity.

This is a skill that leaders such as yourself innately have: being able to look at the landscape and talent and put the right people in the right roles. But do your people have the same skill? They're put on teams and given very few tools to understand the dynamics of the team. You need to share a few tools with them to achieve a better outcome.

Teach them how to do a SWOT analysis of each team member. Identify the individuals' Strengths, Weaknesses, Opportunities, and Threats. An example for "Mary": Strong communication skills, Weak listening skills, Opportunity for training others, Threat that if we don't manage her poor communication skills, she'll disrupt the team. When we teach our people to break down talent into these four dimensions, they can see the dynamics and leverage opportunities while mitigating any potential issues.

You can also implement a VAULT (Value Assessment, Understand, Launch, Test) development plan, which enables you to see opportunities in moving people into different roles. The Value Assessment asks what they are passionate about doing versus what they're currently doing. An example could be a person who is a technical leader on a team who spends more of their time teaching than effectively leading projects. They're seen as a poor performer who is unable to manage the dynamics. Rather than coaching for improvement, could we use this person as a trainer of new technical talent? That would play to the person's strengths and passion and pay respect to them as a human being. They may soon become a high performer. In this development plan, we sought to Understand the value a team member brought to the organization, and through a well-defined Launch into the new role along with a period of Testing and fine-tuning, we created a new role that provided value to the organization.

Feedback Is a Gift, But We Don't Know How to Ask for it

Teach effective feedback skills. Have your mentee banish the question "How am I doing?" because people will provide non-value-added feedback such as "fine" or "let me get back to you." A better approach would be "What should I continue? What should I start doing? What should I change?" A simple change in approach enables people to think about feedback that will be valuable. When we ask what should be *continued*, we are looking for the qualities that make us valuable and that will support our performance should they persist. When we ask what should be *started*, we are looking for the qualities that will enhance what we are already doing well. If a person is already good at presentation skills, starting to weave in storytelling will enhance that strength. When we ask what should be *changed*, we want to know the qualities that have been detracting from what we are doing well. If a person shifts their weight from side to side while speaking, they may want to find a way to reduce their movement, like leaning on a podium.

Going back to the technical leader who has asked for feedback in this way, you could say the following: "You're a great communicator and you should continue to lead with this skill and teach others what you do. You might want to start thinking about a new role in training that will leverage your unique skills in articulating difficult concepts in an easy-to-understand way. I propose that you change the way you show frustration to others when they don't perform in favor of taking those conversations offline."

Helping People to Extract Past and Pride from Team Members Is Teaching Effective Networking Skills

In our past chapters we discussed the CEO's compass points of Past (culture) and Pride (humanity and intellectual property). But have we ever taught this to our team, and truly, what is the impact of these conversations? These are the essential skills of networking—some people have them and some simply don't. We find that the people who don't have these skills are often awkward at social gatherings and we label them as introverts. But are they really? Perhaps we've not given them the skills to launch a dialog of discovery and building trust. A few simple questions can help them learn how to network and build trust—essential for team dynamics.

"My name is Mary; I'd love to learn more about you and the work you're most proud of." (Pride)

"My name is Tom and I'm excited to meet you. Can you tell me more about where you're from and what you enjoy doing?" (Past)

"Welcome to the team, we're excited to have you. Please share with us more about some of your past accomplishments and how you like to spend your free time." (Past and Pride)

As leaders, we have an obligation to model the behavior we want our teams to exhibit. If we instead assume people are what we expect, we are often later blindsided by misunderstandings.

However, what if everyone understood how past and pride were critical to getting on track from the start—wouldn't this potentially avoid conflict later? I propose to you that teaching people these compass points is an investment in time well spent. This can be modeled when you lead meetings or can be a development opportunity during 1-2-1s with individuals.

Conflict Resolution Framework: Helping to Create a Conversation for Alignment

Full transparency here: I AVOID conflict, and that's why I've had to develop the skills (or crutches) to help me through this and guide others. Avoiding conflict may have been one of my pitfalls,

> *Fear not conflict, for facing the fear is the greatest victory.*

as was evidenced when I failed to provide feedback to a subpar employee and later had to fire them for poor performance. It was most likely due to my poor performance in the context of feedback and addressing conflict. Think about your own situation and ask yourself how you handle conflict. If you're adept at this skill, how are your people at this?

One of the things I've learned is that we don't provide a framework for people to have conversations that are constructive and mitigate conflict. We often think about conflict in the context of going into battle because it's bad and has to be crushed. When we as leaders can provide a step-by-step framework to follow, those who have not evolved those skills can slowly build them through practice.

The one piece of advice I would propose to you as you mentor others in this process and you see the discomfort the person has going into the situation is to ask them the question, "What would it look like if you're successful?" This is a point I brought up previously that is a trigger to open up one's mindset from a negative/evasive perspective to one of possibility. It can build confidence in a novice.

I have found that having a conversation plan for such engagement is a tremendous tool to coach people who struggle with these situations.

- Identify the person you want to align with.
- Visualize the outcome you want to achieve.
- Approach the person and address the situation where there is a gap in understanding that is causing the conflict.
- Agree on the gap that exists (avoid making it personal).
- Present a grounding statement that breaks the tension and aligns individuals.
- Seek understanding in why there is a gap.
- Agree to actions on both sides to close the gap.

Examples of grounding statements may include:

- Do we agree that "X" is important?
- Here's the situation "X" and the gap "Y" that needs to be addressed.

And here's an example of **moving to resolution**:

- Now that we agree on the gap, I'll take this action. Would it make sense if you took this action?

The Process of Building a High-Performing Team Leaves a Lasting Impact

I know firsthand what it looks like to build a high-performing team, and it has nothing to do with having the best talent. Dysfunction can happen even with the smartest people in the room if they don't have effective team skills. Rather than discuss in detail how I cultivated my team, I'd rather show you what "peace of mind" looks like when the process works. After each of these examples I share with you, close your eyes and think about whether you've seen this in your workplace. If yes, you're on the path to peace of mind. If not, then the tools in this chapter are highly recommended.

Thinkers vs. Doers

"Deb, there's a quality issue in the plant with a potential service impact. I'm gathering the team to do a deep dive and will keep you posted."

"Do you need anything from me?"

"No, I'm good, but I know I can come back to you with my proposals and we can discuss solutions."

Resolving Conflict by Seeking Common Ground

"Tom, help me to understand why you don't see this issue as urgent? We need your support."

"I see the issue as urgent, but it can be handled at the plant level and does not require escalation at this point."

"Okay, I see the difference. Then can you commit to notifying the senior staff and I'll manage the issue in the plant?

Do I have your commitment to get involved if we reach the next level of urgency?"

"Of course; keep me posted while I inform the senior team."

When Strength and Passion Create Pride

"I'm so glad I moved out of the plant role and now teach problem-solving and root cause analysis. It combines my love for history, curiosity about how and why things happen, and the opportunity to help people with critical thinking. I really love what I do."

As you move along the journey of coaching performance in your team, take the time to pause and reflect about that transformation you've seen and use these questions as part of your 1-2-1s to improve individual and team performance.

Self-Reflection

- What behaviors have you taken on?
- What behaviors have you stopped doing?

Peer Feedback

- What are people saying about you?
- How has their behavior changed around you?

Closing Thought

The process of investing in your team's dynamics is an enabler for peace of mind. Knowing what I've shared with you and how it can be instrumental to getting you back on track, what are the next steps for you? Do you have the capacity or capability to teach this to your team? Is there someone in your organization who is good at this whom you can partner with to elevate your team's performance? If you still do not have that resource you can leverage, do you have a network you can tap into to help you? Take some time to think about this, because if this is the compass point that has you off track, now would be a good time to think about how to leverage resources to steer you in the right direction.

CHAPTER 9

Compass Point: Platform Tools that Elevate Your Team's Impact

When Following the Platform Compass Point Will Take You Off Course

While I'm not a proponent of providing insights about what NOT to do, I'd be remiss not to caution you about how not to steer in the platform direction. What I mean by this is that often the response to a problem is to implement a new tool when the foundation is unstable and we aren't leading from a human-centric approach. The best way to share what I mean is the following example that describes what NOT to do and what works better.

Lead with Platform and Crash the Ship

Faced with a rapid integration, the critical path item was to move the acquired sites onto the main ERP (Enterprise Resource Planning) system. Given the complexity, the team was led by IT with supporting functions engaged. I saw gaps in a holistic approach to this strategy, including in such areas as gaining input from internal and external stakeholders, mapping critical processes, and understanding resource needs. The implementation team respectfully acknowledged these gaps, but did not prioritize them for action. The team successfully flipped the switch on time, but later realized issues that prevented the system from shipping the product to customers. Needless to say, the customers were paralyzed and brand loyalty was quickly eroding.

In another workstream, quality professionals were mapped from the current state to the new resource structure, customers were contacted to understand their unique specifications, and in the face of challenges, the plants knew whom to go to, to resolve issues. During that time, there were no disruptions in quality, and where there were discrepancies, the issues were quickly resolved.

What was different? Starting the project by understanding the past, pride, and people gave us a foundation that allowed us to integrate capability and capacity. Closing those gaps first and then proceeding with platform solutions led to the success of this workstream.

This sounds so simple, but behind the scenes we used numerous platform tools to give the organization what they needed to go through rapid transformation. Especially with rapid transformation, we find that leading with tools only is a bad strategy. We find that gaps quickly reveal themselves in terms of capacity and capability. Tools are needed to get people back on track and to sustainably stay on course. The next part will give you tools to use platform successfully in conjunction with the other compass points.

Time Management: Knowing the Difference Between What Is Important, Urgent, and Somewhere in Between.

In my work, I've seen an interesting phenomenon happen especially with high performers or people you're coaching and who are responding to your feedback. It's a battle for them to prioritize their work because they lack good prioritization and time management skills. Here are a few symptoms I've found both in myself as well as in emerging talent.

When the individual starts to stand out as a more valuable resource, they begin to get a lot of emails, requests for their time, and more meetings. These demands on a person's time are both a reward and a curse for their new presence, confidence, and leadership.

- They're excited about the new attention they're getting, but lack good prioritization skills for understanding how to best allocate their time.
- They think they're invincible and that their reward will come from accomplishing more tasks or overextending themselves.
- They appear to be successful by getting more work done, but later they may burn out.
- Even when they have good prioritization skills, they may need tools to hold them accountable to deadlines.

I know you're a busy leader and would hope that over time, someone would have shown them these skills. Surely, you think your leadership has these skills and should be cascading them to the rest of their team. But I ask you the hard question: do they really have these vital tools and are they able to help the team? If not, it may be a matter of time until you see the results manifest in burnout and disengagement. So, I ask that you take the time to really evaluate if the tools and platforms are really stable to enable your people to manage their time and priorities.

One of the best tools I've found is the "Eisenhower Matrix," which breaks down work content into Urgent and Important as follows:

- Urgent and Important—Do Now
- Not Urgent but Important—Schedule
- Urgent but Not Important—Delegate
- Not Urgent and Not Important—Delete

In my last corporate job, I received feedback that I had poor decision logic and prioritization. With no coaching (don't let this be you!), I found an online course that included the Eisenhower Matrix. With no follow-up or coaching, I slowly had to develop this muscle—and, I might add, as an entrepreneur it is so very difficult to delegate or delete! Even now, it's a constant struggle not to chase the squirrel or shiny penny. I'm an expert in the making, but if you had to ask yourself the hard question "how good am I at prioritizing" and be honest with the answer, what would you say? If you struggle, perhaps your people do as well. Steer the ship quickly by checking the health of your team's decision logic and prioritization. Stop now: the rest of the tools I discuss will only be successful if your team has these prerequisites.

Active Listening: The Ultimate Superpower

We think we know how to listen, but when we observe our team **reacting** to what was **said** rather than. **responding** to what was **heard**, we see a dynamic that will be slow to achieve an outcome. The subtle difference is based on our use of time to process in-

> *Listen with compassion, see beyond what is seen, and feel deeply to understand the human spirit.*

formation. Active listening is the art of deeply listening to the words that are said, making an emotional and intellectual connection to the human, and reframing and repeating what was heard to convey that the message was understood. If your people don't have this, you're missing an opportunity to build the ultimate in individual and team performance.

This topic is important because

- When you practice deep listening, it shows a person you heard them.
- When you can reframe what you heard, the person immediately forms a deep connection with you as if you're singing from the same sheet of music.
- When you see both heads nodding in unison, you see a bond and partnership that is based on trust and connection.

We often struggle with this skill because people tend to process what they hear in terms of how it affects them. We have to develop a skill that is like a tape recorder to play it back in our mind like a *Reader's Digest* version of what the other party meant. It's not about what you hear, it's about what was intended. This is very different. In order to have an influence, you need to move people within their world, not yours.

I propose that you follow this simple rule: start from a place of reframing instead of responding or reacting.

Let's imagine you're having a conversation with a colleague who is very upset about world affairs. Most people would like to respond or react with their own opinion. A better way that demonstrates active listening might be:

"So, if I understand what you said, the entire political landscape is bothersome and you just wish we could get back to work."

The person responds, "Exactly!" Then you say, "So, given that's where we need to go, what is something that you can do that would bring some normalcy to your routine?"

Note, this is a very influential conversation where you hear a person talking about their frustration and not being able to move forward because they feel consumed by world affairs. By reframing, it shows that you heard them, and if you offer them something that is in their control, you short-circuit a never-ending, non-serving loop.

Do you have powerful active listening skills? Who on you team does, and can they mentor others to improve this skill? If your team is actively responding and reacting to conversations, who is going to guide them to better active listening? It's a worthy question, and investment in this tool can build a higher-performing team.

Coaching New Levels of Performance

My experience in Lean and Six Sigma process improvement methodology taught me the most important thing to remember after you've improved some level of performance is to implement control measures. In the context of mentoring your team and giving them the tools to improve their performance, all too often I've seen a new behavior regress due to external or internal triggers, and we need to avoid that.

I once had a client share that since they'd been invited into so many new projects because of their elevated image, people were starting to micromanage their work. This is very typical of leaders who feel they're losing control of people who are starting to outshine them and so they revert to retaining control instead of developing their people. In this moment, my client was starting to lose their confidence, indicating that their behaviors were not solidified at the new level of performance.

It's important to protect your investments in developing your people and helping them to find tools to emphasize their higher level of performance until it becomes a habit. In this case, I shared the accountability tool I developed to help them continue to practice their new behaviors until the habit was solidified and no amount of external input would impact the new level of performance.

Over the years, was there a new skill you had to develop where you wish someone had given you the tools needed to make it easier? Your mentee's new "normal" is still very new and your leadership is critical to sustaining the gains.

> *You have all the power you need. Don't give it away.*

Managing Power and Position

The topic of power and position might be considered something reserved for senior leadership training, but I propose that the subtleties of these topics can make or break an evolving team dynamic.

- As the leadership capability of your team grows, they will get more opportunity to be responsible—a level of power because people trust them.
- With power comes the new responsibility to elevate others and give them the tools they need to do the work and be trusted.
- With new power comes other challenges—other people may want to control you more because you've gained more power.

I have found the RACI tool to be excellent at leveling the playing field when team dynamics start to manifest power plays that could impact the growth of the people on your team. This simple tool asks that you break you team into the following roles.

Responsible: The team member assigned to complete a task.

Accountable: This person delegates the work to the Responsible person and has the ultimate sign-off that the work is complete.

Consulted: This person is consulted for their input that could set the direction of the tasks to be completed.

Inform: These people simply need to be kept in the loop and advised of progress.

This tool is highly powerful for aiding an individual in setting the roles at the beginning of a project, establishing a new procedure, or "dropping" into a chaotic situation and establishing baseline expectations of individuals.

When we reflect back to the situation where an evolving individual was being micromanaged by their leader, it may be that the leader's role is simply to be "informed" and not "accountable." When these roles are clearly defined, the person you're coaching regains their power and control. You've given them a tool that qualifies the respective positions on the team; from there, they can steer the ship back on course.

Powerful Messaging for Impact

How often have you heard someone on your team say to you after a meeting: "I'm so frustrated! I showed them the data, but I couldn't get them to understand it was important to purchase that new equipment." To make matters worse, you start to see their negative mindset come forward in a self-fulfilling prophesy that they can't influence others and they simply don't understand them. It may be a symptom of something far greater—we've not given them the tools for powerful messaging.

> *Pick powerful words and speak with methodical confidence. You will then realize your impact and relevance.*

This issue is further exacerbated by social norms that profile you if you pick words that are too aggressive or too weak. Unless we mentor our people on the proper selection of words and how they can impact an outcome, we've failed to equip them with the tools needed to carry out their work.

My powerful phrase bank includes

- "I propose"
- "We need"
- "I believe"
- "I know"

Avoid at all costs these phrases:

- "I think"
- "I hope"
- "Do we"
- "Should we"

When we combine these powerful phrases into a conversation map such as

- What is the current state?
- What change is needed?
- What is the call to action?

then we give our people the framework to communicate a powerful message and decrease their frustration.

Here are some "Bad" and "Better" examples to depict what I mean and what you should be watching your team doing:

Bad: The number of internal rejections is increasing; we think the operators are not following instructions and we need to form a team.

Better: A key indicator of process control is the number of internal rejections, and we're realizing an increasing trend over the last three months. Based on the data, the biggest opportunity is in developing standards for training so we can have repeatable results and decrease internal rejections. I propose we form a team to prioritize the standards and an execution plan to get three new standards complete by the end of the month.

Bad: The inventory levels are increasing to their highest level since 2019. We have to put limits on our purchasing department. If we don't do this, we won't meet our budget numbers. (Throwing gas onto the fire without providing solutions.)

Better: Inventory levels have exceeded our target, and I propose we define purchasing standards to manage the limits of purchasing to ensure we stay within budget without impacting consumption.

Communication and Connection: Has Your Team Mastered This?

Have you ever tried to listen to someone with a different accent and found it hard to understand them? Have you ever tried to listen to a conversation in a different language, but could only understand 40 percent? Have you listened to someone of high intelligence, but found you did not understand the technical terminology? If this is you, you are not alone, because when most people speak, it's to be heard but not understood.

About nine years ago, I was teaching Six Sigma Green Belt continuous improvement methodology at a beautiful resort in Spain with the Mediterranean Sea in the background (sigh!). I had the good fortune of co-leading the content with another experienced instructor who had charisma and knowledge far deeper than I had at the time. He had taken me under his wing and I was grateful for the opportunity to travel, learn new cultures, and grow my skills in training others.

However, the experience had both a weakness and an opportunity that I was able to take advantage of. The primary instructor spoke in American English, which has many expressions that are not common to non-English speaking people, and our audience was international. Many people were polite and nodded their heads in understanding, but that was simply to keep the presentation moving along. Because the content was a little challenging for me, I took a position of speaking in very simple and concise English so I was sure I would not make a mistake. What happened next was important, so stick with me!

During a break, I was approached by some of the students who shared how much they enjoyed the class. They proceeded in saying that while they respected the main instructor, they found it difficult to understand him. They had to translate the information into their primary language while processing the technical information. Where frequent slang was used, they could not understand the content. When I spoke, the translation was very easy and they really understood the content much better. Their thanks made me very happy, and now I realize how important the lesson in that moment was, and I carry that forward to my work.

I understood my audience first, and then my job was to seek to be understood by them. When we start from a place of caring about humanity, the way we connect takes on a whole new meaning.

With this in mind, how can you start communications from a place of humanity and ensure that you're understood?

If you are a business leader who sees your team having challenges in connecting with people, ask yourself if it is in the way they communicate. It's your responsibility to ensure that those who work for you are seen, heard, and respected and that they have the tools needed to connect. After all, they're a reflection of your leadership and you have a duty to ensure your team can lead effectively through the words they use and how others connect with them.

If any of this sounds familiar, I ask you to pause and reflect if you're equipped with the skills and time to evolve how you connect with humanity. An investment in yourself and the people you serve can go a long way toward having you be heard and understood.

Have You Set Your Team Up for Success with the Right Tools and Platforms for Performance?

This is a good stopping point to reflect on all the tools I've shared with you, and please know this is only a small sample of what I offer my clients. Most of these are actionable straight out of this book and are probably quite familiar to you. The challenge may be finding the time to mentor your team with these new skills, and even more importantly as you look at your team down the ranks, considering whether they all have the capability and capacity to build these skills. Remember, as I shared in earlier chapters, every employee has the potential to be a high performer. Can you build these skills in all of them? Let's back down on that and, instead, ask if you can evolve this with your direct reports at a minimum. If not, think about how you'll get the capacity to focus on this compass point if you believe it will have a major impact on getting you back on track. When you're done, I'll see you in Chapter 10: Performance.

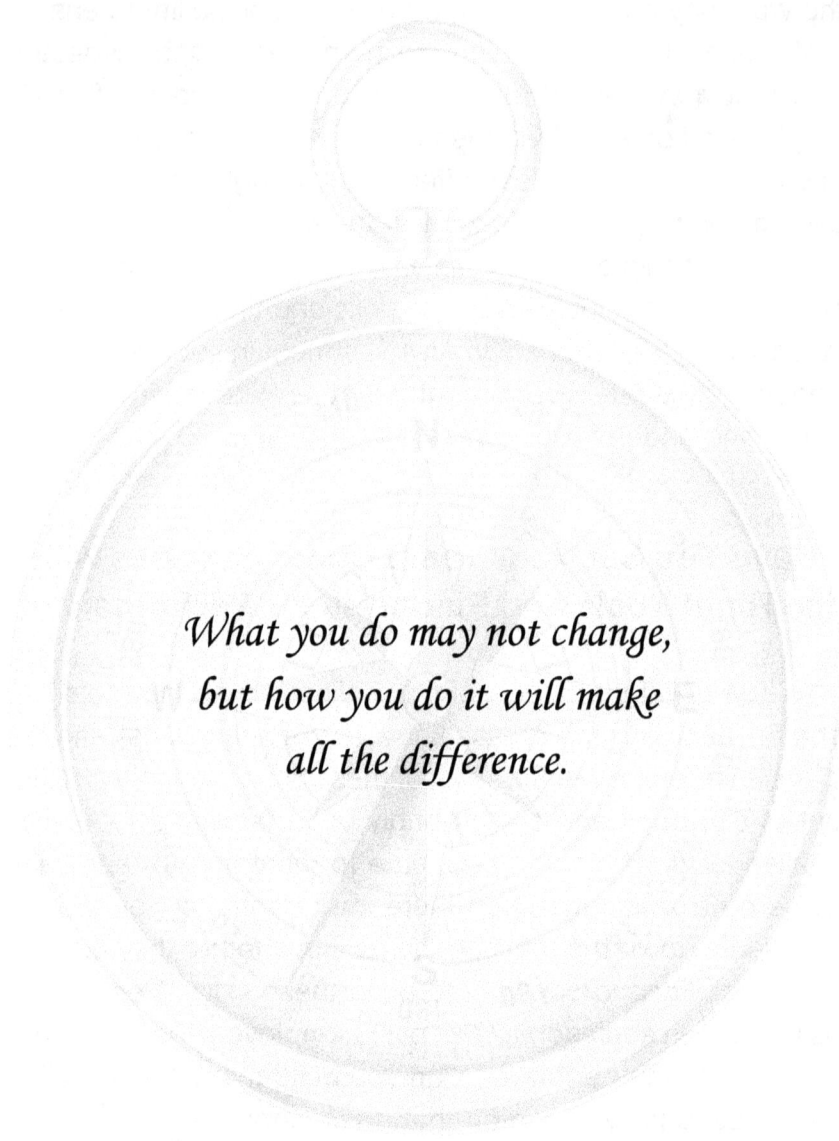

What you do may not change,
but how you do it will make
all the difference.

CHAPTER 10

Compass Point: Performance

CEOs should be focused on mentoring and guiding their emerging leaders. When you help build their capabilities in order to let go of tasks you are not suited to do, you're building your succession plan. The CEO needs to build the capability in their direct reports, and this process must be repeated down through the organization. Leveraging the compass point of purpose in conjunction with a strong foundation in people and the process of high-performance teams, we can start to achieve optimal performance and get the results you need. While simple in theory, it becomes a challenge when the next leadership level down lacks the essential skills to develop their direct reports.

I often use the term "Corporate Destabilization" to describe the outcome of promoting people into positions that they are not equipped for. The problem festers if ignored, and when organizations go through rapid change, the foundation starts to crumble. If we set up a proactive approach to address essential skills and performance at all levels of the organization, we stabilize the foundation.

Now I have to ask you a hard question: What's preventing you from developing the next layer?

I don't have time—I'm focused on other priorities in the business.

- I only have time to work on the Star Performers.
- It's faster/better if I do myself; others simply don't have this skill and I need to get critical work done now. I'll get to it tomorrow.

It's someone else's job—I know it's important, but it's not my strength.

- I'll hand it off to HR.
- We'll send them out for classes to develop skills.
- We've hired a consultant and they've provided training.

They've been here so long—they can't be changed.

- We'll hire someone to bridge the gap.
- We'll wait until they retire and then replace with a different set of skills.
- Let's move them to an assignment where they won't bother anyone.

These behaviors result in a legacy of avoidance rather than leading and building a culture of courage to get back on track.

Before I share how to resolve these problems, let me share a story about how I failed and see if this resonates with you or someone else who's performance has not been developed.

Ascending to Leadership Too Early and Without Mentoring

At thirty-five, I had the role of Director of Quality with a staff of twelve for a startup optical networking company, and I had arrived—or so I thought. Let's take it back three years. I had come in as employee number sixty with a staff of five, and soon the company grew to 500 and was getting ready to go public. I had ascended to the role of director after being the manager of quality and having the courage to pitch my promotion to the president of the company. I had even been complimented on how so few people can advocate for themselves because they only advocate for their employees. I felt truly accomplished at this point in my career. And then the leadership changed and so did my life.

Most of my hires were self-starters in the area of quality who intrinsically knew what the job was and came to me with well thought-out suggestions or enhancements to the organization. These people were clearly at a higher maturity level than most, and again, I felt so fortunate. However, one hire was a good performer but they did not get along with everyone. I saw this but chose to ignore it because we were getting the results we wanted.

However, as time passed, the ability for this worker to productively engage with others was deteriorating, and at the same time, I was not providing mentoring to understand the situation and work through the issues. Concurrently, those who saw the challenges of this person in the organization were not mentoring me on the situation and how to address it. Ultimately, I was asked by my leadership to let the person go, and this is where it gets to the crux of the issue.

With human resources as my backstop, I delivered the bad news that it just wasn't working out. The person was taken aback, and while they realized they were having challenges with people in the organization, they said, "Just tell me what to do." I knew at that point we were well beyond any performance improvement plan as the decision had already been made to let them go. However, in the moment, the pain was excruciating for both of us as the person's reality was changing. Concurrently, I was not equipped to deliver the message because I had been given a script with no skills to navigate a difficult conversation.

With the message delivered, as I exited the room to leave the employee with HR to discuss their exit as a well-choreographed dance, I felt completely lost. Not only did I feel bad about letting someone go, but I also felt lost about not having the skills to manage this. First, I'd had no skills to coach performance for the individual. Second, there had been no forum for me to meet with my manager to discuss the situation and ways to get back on track. In fact, the leadership had changed and I did not have monthly 1-2-1s to discuss such issues. Essentially, I had been left on an island to do the deed of exiting someone from the business without the benefit of developing skills to either prevent or manage the issue.

Talk about a low point to my career, but I got through it—and then this happened. The company continued to grow and I wanted to revise the organizational structure to set it up for long-term success. I submitted the proposal to my boss on several occasions, seeking to align and gain their feedback. They didn't respond at first and continued to avert any engagement with me; again, I felt lost. Here I was trying to put forth a new idea with justification and it appeared not to be important to the organization. There's nothing worse than going through the day and feeling unsupported. And then I ask you, are there people in your organization who may be going through the same thing? Feeling lost, unsupported, and not receiving the benefit of your leadership, lessons learned, and mentoring?

This story did not end well, but did ultimately lead me to an organization that did engage in building a high-performance organization that not only focused on the business strategy and tactical performance, but made people performance a critical part of their leadership responsibility. I've since had the good fortune of working for many such companies, and with that, I share some thoughts for your consideration.

Feedback Without Support Breaks the Individual Spirit

Ten years ago, I was in a meeting with my boss and corporate quality leaders to discuss the hiring of a new quality engineer who would replace me as I moved into a new role in the organization. The leaders were discussing the qualifications that were needed for this role, and I was not in alignment with the direction they were taking. I spoke up and said "Isn't this an operations role and not a corporate quality role?" In the next moment, the absolute silence felt like an eternity. I don't remember how the conversation ended, but I know I spoke up and it was not taken well.

Sometime later, my boss called me into his office and told me "You shouldn't have said that." What I don't remember is any coaching I got about what would have been a better approach. I can only remember the moment of devastation—"You shouldn't have said that." Whatever happened during the meeting where I spoke up and the follow-up meeting is a blur, but hearing nothing and then getting admonished had an impact for many years. I stopped speaking up and voicing my opinion, and instead I played it safe.

I ultimately left that organization because they were no longer supporting my growth to impact on a greater scale, which I did find in another company. The new company allowed me to take risks, show my technical potential, and grow my essential skills.

How can we change the trend for both the individual and the leaders who are not prepared to manage these situations and who are causing more devastation?

Why Can't Everyone Be a High Performer?

This may be an unpopular opinion, but everyone can be an emerging leader and can be mentored. If they're not capable of being a high performer, then ask yourself: do I have the right people on the team? Do we settle for Steady Eddies because the short game is they get the work done? Are you settling? If you're new to an organization or taking a step back to reflect on what could be done differently with respect to your talent, let's start with a few thoughts for your consideration.

1. **Everyone is a High Performer.** Start with that mindset and things start to change. You instantly instill confidence in everyone. Some high performers stand out in a crowd and absolutely should be cultivated for higher and higher levels of responsibility. But roll up your sleeves and spend the time getting to know

everyone and their unique gifts. You may find some high performers are in "stealth mode" and are simply not visible. You may find they're critical and need to be on your radar. And let's not forget those with the reputation of being poor performers—people will tell you about them as well. But for some reason, no one has taken the time to really get to know them, their unique strengths, and whether they're potentially in the wrong role or lack mentorship to bring forth what they're meant to do. I realize it's a lot of work, but why not challenge the "bell-shaped curve" and consider that everyone can be a high performer?

2. **At the business level:** Discuss the purpose/vision/ mission and very clearly articulate the alignment of every function to it. I sincerely ask that you consider doing this more than once a year. People get busy with work, and we should take the time to remind people what is important. I don't recommend walking over to where you have this message posted on the wall and reading it to your people, but discuss the essence of the purpose of the company and align people with it, especially during challenging times. More importantly, I suggest doing it in the context of the skills needed in the organization to align with the purpose. Integrate the development of essential skills as part of a business level objective.

Let's say that the vision for the company is to be the partner of choice in your industry. Do your people truly understand what that means? For a salesperson, it may be obviously tied to their win rate, but what does that mean for the shipping worker—how do they manifest their role in "becoming the partner of choice"? Could it mean their role is to ensure that the product gets to the customer on time and provide a great experience?

An example could be that the shipping worker calls the customer's receiving personnel and confirms the product was received on time and in good condition. Does this person have the skills for such a conversation with your customer? Do the shipping personnel see their role as an integral part of the overall vision? If not, take a moment to think about how your messaging is getting down and across all people in your organization and whether you have equipped them with the right skills. If the answer is no, are you truly leading with purpose and achieving the organizational performance you need?

3. **At the team level, start every project/activity by discussing essential skills,** before strategic work and tactical details. This could be as simple as asking "What went well? What did not go well? What could be improved in the team dynamic?" Start with mentoring as an integral part of the team's work before moving on to strategic and tactical work. If we start from a place of reflection on team performance, we can focus on the big picture and short-circuit any tendency to leap directly to the minutia of the meeting or phone call or shipment they were previously engaged with. When we bring people together to conduct purposeful work, we need their minds to be present.

This also demonstrates to them that you care about the human first and not simply the task at hand. You are mentoring in the moment as the team discusses what behaviors to continue, what to start doing, and what others to change in favor of better performance.

Out of that could come some actions focused on individual or team performance.

I once had an employee who had a terrible time getting started with a project that they had the essential skills to lead but lacked the tactical skills for. The result was they were procrastinating. When asked for the status of this project during a staff meeting, they admitted they simply didn't know how to get started and needed some help. That quickly showed me there was a gap in capability, and we agreed to meet offline to outline the tactical steps. Once we met and walked through the steps, instantaneously their confidence came back and they said, "I got this!" When we make mentoring an integral part of team and individual capability, it becomes part of our culture instead of an isolated event in the output of a performance review.

4. **At the individual level:** Monthly 1-2-1s are focused on individual skill development first and then the strategic and tactical elements of their work. But before we go any further, do you have monthly 1-2-1s with your direct reports? Forgive, me, but I don't want to hear that you talk every day. I want you to think hard about whether you set aside time away from the day-to-day to have a 1-2-1. If not, you're missing out on so much with your employee.

   Unless you have a highly mature culture where mentoring is an ongoing activity, these meetings are most likely not happening. It's critical to your organization's success to be having regular time set aside to communicate about performance as well as having a system of productive feedback to improve essential skills. This is an investment in improving performance before it becomes a liability when unattended. During this time, we build skills in giving and receiving feedback, and I might suggest a method that has been highly successful for myself.

Try an approach around (a) what to continue (plays to strengths), (b) what to start (ways to enhance what they're already doing well) and (c) what to change (things to perhaps stop doing so they do not detract from good work). I have found this invaluable, and when done right, it makes performance discussions a positive experience. If you've not experienced this in your mentorship or by mentoring others, I assure you this will change the experience completely.

A Manager Becomes a Leader Because of 1-2-1 Mentoring

I had a highly skilled quality leader on my team who was quite an authority. He was the go-to person who bailed me out of some really challenging quality issues we encountered. At one training session, he decided to stand while delivering a presentation, and what I saw completely floored me. Not only did people listen to this person, they were leaning into what he said. He was not only the subject matter expert, but he also exuded power and authority. It was truly remarkable to see what was already a strength become a superpower.

During our next 1-2-1, I asked how he felt about that event. He said he felt pretty good and hoped his message had gotten through. When I shared with him to (a) **continue** to present his knowledge, but also to (b) **start** standing when he spoke for all future events, he thanked me for that feedback, and from that point on, even if he was doing a presentation within the confines of his office, he stood to provide a more powerful message.

So, in this case, the person already had a strength in public speaking, and providing them the feedback to stand enhanced something they were already doing well.

Ask yourself if you take the time to provide such feedback to your team. Even more importantly, are your team members with direct reports providing the same framework to mentor and provide feedback to those reports on a regular basis? If not, what's holding them back?

How Do You Assess Your Level of Organizational Maturity in This Area?

After all, this is a chapter on performance, right? In my work with organizations, there are a series of Leading and Lagging indicators that I've implemented to evaluate the current state and areas for improvement. I propose Leading indicators as areas of focus where you need to improve your "performance" compass point. These principles are integral to human-centric leadership.

Leading Indicators (focus most of your time here)

- % leaders conducting monthly 1-2-1s
- % employees who can explain the purpose of the organization in the context of their role
- % employees who have developed a competency in a new skill in their current or new role
- % people engaged in a mentor/mentee relationship
- % people asked to leverage their new skill in a new role or project

Lagging indicators are the traditional metrics that leaders look at as indicators of health in managing human capital. They simply measure activity and don't measure the impact of performance.

Lagging Indicators (measure these, but don't spend too much time here)

- % people promoted
- % employee retention
- % trained in essential skills
- % performance reviews done on time
- % satisfied with organizational culture

Within this framework of managing performance at the business, team, and individual levels, you start to see that it is possible for everyone to be a high performer. If we set the stage for aligning with the purpose, assuring connectivity of each department/individual to the purpose, and then evolving the essential skills at all levels, everyone is moving forward together at their highest potential. Ask yourself if your organization is worth that kind of investment. Would you make the time? Would you ensure that support people charged with this effort see this as a mission-critical part of the business success? Could even the people whom you don't think you can change potentially evolve under this framework?

If you've adopted this framework and the people on your team still do not respond, have you asked yourself whether you have the wrong people on your team?

I'm done asking all the questions for now. While I'd love to engage with you in a conversation, now is the time for you to start asking yourself these questions. Go back through the chapter and review all the questions. If you're not on track with the organization's performance because you've not invested enough time on personnel development, what will you do differently now? If you can't steer the ship and implement all the suggestions in this chapter, what is one thing you can do starting now?

If you're struggling and can't answer this right now, I suggest you put down the book and simply pause. There's no reason to continue if you don't have the answer to achieve ultimate performance of people in your business. You'll never get to peace of mind if we can't get this course corrected. When you have asked yourself a few questions and have a few actionable steps to start doing now, pick up the book again and proceed to the next chapter. I'll be there for you.

What do your clients really need?
Our experience services them functionally,
but connecting with them emotionally
gives them trust and that little
something extra that is more
valuable—peace of mind.

CHAPTER 11

The CEO's Compass: How The System Works Together

Take a breath and pause, because we're about to show you how this all works together. This is your time to see the framework and ask yourself what your current state is and where you are off track. Remember, true north is peace of mind, where you want to steer the ship back on track. The opportunities in your organization can be one or many of the compass points—often not all of them—hence why this is not delivered as a "eight-step" approach like many guides. This is your opportunity to think for yourself and decide which areas to focus on and which are foundationally under control.

What I have found in many instances is that two or three areas need to be worked on, and I'll share a few scenarios to illustrate how we got some organizations back on track. In the end, it is for you to determine what is needed, and I can guide the process.

Purpose: Creating systems that establish a sense of purpose that guides the ship and is clearly visible throughout the organization in modeled behavior

Past: Leadership understanding culture and bringing it forward as part of building trust within the team and enabling team dynamics

Strategic

Tactical

Process: In the context of team dynamics; Developing critical thinking, conflict management, powerful messaging & feedback

Platform: also know as Tools needed in the context of human development and self management including: accountability, time management, decision Logic, Strategic planning skills

Peace of Mind

Purpose

Past

The CEO's Compass

Process

Platform

Performance

Pride

People

Peace of Mind: Stability, Scalable, Customer Advocacy and Customer Partnership

Performance: Leading and Lagging indicators of organization maturity

Pride: Intersection of People & their Intellectual property, gifts and expertise. Critical to get people on board as part of the team.

People: Mentoring individuals to Build Essential Skills, Mindset, Communication skills for impact and giving & receiving feedback.

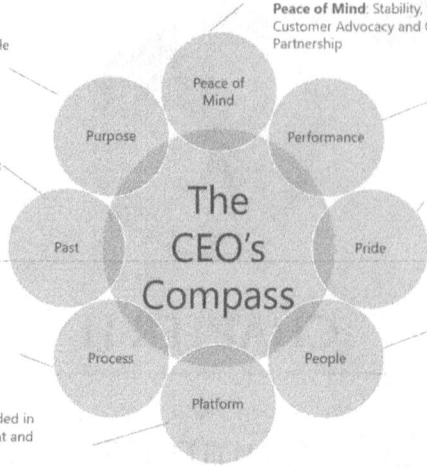

Case 1: Strong Strategic Foundation, but Lacking Tactical Elements for Growth

I love my work, especially first encounters with CEOs and senior business leaders — the gentle dance of getting to know one another and the organizational challenges they're facing. They may not be forthcoming at first, but after some well-placed questions, you'll start to see a picture forming of a leader off track. It's nothing to do with their past experience or capability in the current state, but simply the set of cards they were dealt, especially if they've recently arrived on the scene.

In this one case, I could see tremendous pride coming through as they smiled about the intellectual property the company was founded on and the deep culture of "can do" attitudes throughout the ranks. While the company was still evolving, there was an inherent culture of people organizing around the issue of the day and getting through it. They were mission-focused on customer satisfaction, as are most low-maturity organizations because it's so easy to focus on quality and service. This wonderful foundation built on their past and pride was a great position for them to be in. Their sense of purpose brought them together at times of calm and also of crisis.

But this can be a detriment as an organization changes under your leadership or in response to circumstances, and what served as a strong foundation in the past starts to crumble and chaos ensues. What we find at these junctures is that a lack of tactical organizational maturity, in terms of individual people's capability and the interactions between people and the process, starts to erode the success of the past. Silos and conflicts start to appear that if left unmanaged, lead to adversarial relationships, and the boat starts to rock more. As I cautioned you earlier in this book, do not throw good resources or money after bad because this won't get you back on course. Instead, leverage the platform or tools to enable people to develop the new skills needed to elevate the maturity and accountability of the organization.

When engaging with this leader, we decided on a course of action to shift the quality and operations department's functions, which had been primarily reacting to crises, so they were strategically aligned with the purpose of the organization by integrating their workstreams with those of the compliance, processes, and development departments. During this time, while we kicked off initiatives that would ensure customer satisfaction and trust during rapid growth, we also targeted developing skills in two key individuals in the organization. The team established monthly and weekly 1-2-1s and accountability to the roadmap, and I'm pleased to say they're back on track.

Does this sound familiar to your organization? Have you been very successful, but amid rapid growth, started to see things getting rocky? While the past, pride, and purpose have worked well, are you starting to see the lack of essential skills and team performance have a negative impact? If so, steer your ship to focus on people, process, and platform. While Performance is part of the overall solution, getting the foundational tactical elements started will naturally lead you to the work done in the Performance compass point.

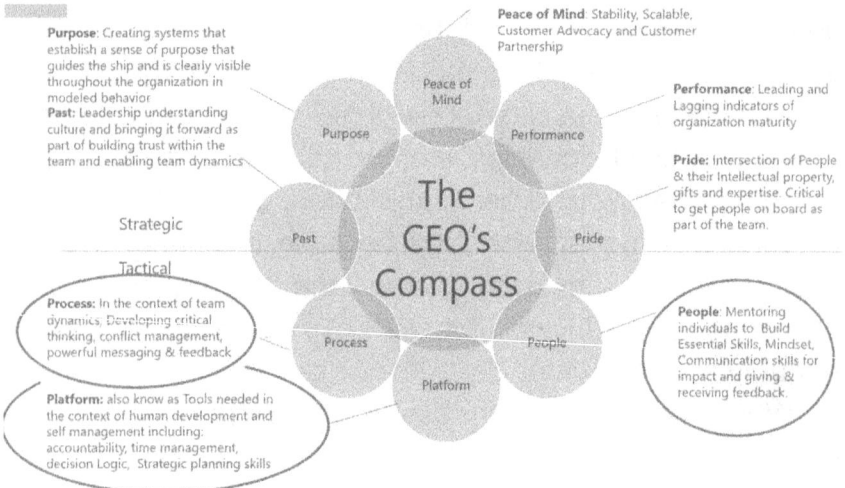

Purpose: Creating systems that establish a sense of purpose that guides the ship and is clearly visible throughout the organization in modeled behavior
Past: Leadership understanding culture and bringing it forward as part of building trust within the team and enabling team dynamics

Strategic

Tactical

Process: In the context of team dynamics; Developing critical thinking, conflict management, powerful messaging & feedback

Platform: also know as Tools needed in the context of human development and self management including: accountability, time management, decision Logic, Strategic planning skills

Peace of Mind: Stability, Scalable, Customer Advocacy and Customer Partnership

Performance: Leading and Lagging indicators of organization maturity

Pride: Intersection of People & their Intellectual property, gifts and expertise. Critical to get people on board as part of the team.

People: Mentoring individuals to Build Essential Skills, Mindset, Communication skills for impact and giving & receiving feedback.

The CEO's Compass

Case 2: Acquiring Mature Resources, but Creating Crisis When Failing to Acquire Their Past and Pride

I wish I didn't have to share the ugly first, but this will grab you. I was part of an acquisition on a very tight timeline and the focus was primarily on technology integration in order to service customers with the new business model. On paper, the technical gurus had a tried-and-true plan, but it went terribly off course and left the customer in a service outage.

There were critical errors made when the time was not taken to understand the acquired company's processes and important touchpoints with their existing customers. As such, when the technical integration took place, valuable pieces of information did not cascade through the systems, leaving the company unable to deliver the product on time and with the right documentation. The hours and hours of wasted time and effort to "rework" the process was devastating to both organizations, and it took a long time to rebuild trust.

There is an upside to this story, as my organization realized we needed to understand more about the people, the processes, their past (culture), and their pride (human and intellectual property) to really understand how to integrate and come out as one in servicing the customer. We learned there were critical pieces of data that were new to our business model as well as expertise we did not have going into the integration. Seeing those gaps, we assembled teams to understand the unique information that the customer depended on before the integration and would need continuing forward.

I often shared that sub-teams were needed across all the other business functions to go through the same process. Unfortunately, these suggestions were acknowledged and parked on a "we'll get to it" list—perhaps that was a bad decision.

Fast forward to what happened when we provided respect to the people and the past and pride they were bringing forward to the integrated organization—we were proud to say there were no disruptions due to quality issues. We understood the new requirements and closed gaps to avert issues. Even when there were minor issues behind the scenes, the new and old organizations came together and were resourceful in solving problems. It is because during the integration we paid respect to people first and the technical solutions second that my division wound up in a better place than the rest of the organization.

So, ask yourself, is this your situation? Do you have a team of great technical resources that by virtue of their culture have great individual and team skills? Are you now taking them on a journey that pushes their limits, expanding or changing the landscape significantly, and seeing things start to break down? Is there something that you can't put your finger on because you're missing some information? Is there something in the backgrounds of the people you were not aware of and now that conflict is starting to show up? Is there missing information that some people have, but you never asked them? When we assume that teams are performing well but we start to transform quickly, we find sometimes that past and pride are the compass points that need attention to get back on track.

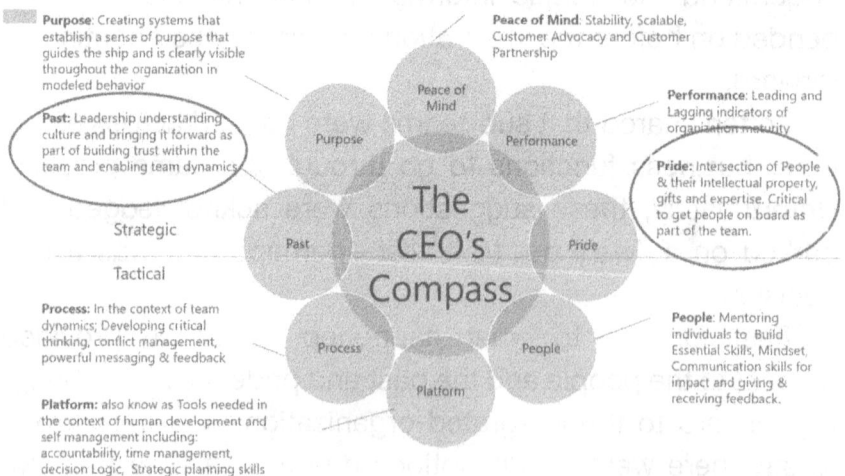

Purpose: Creating systems that establish a sense of purpose that guides the ship and is clearly visible throughout the organization in modeled behavior

Peace of Mind: Stability, Scalable, Customer Advocacy and Customer Partnership

Performance: Leading and Lagging indicators of organization maturity

Past: Leadership understanding culture and bringing it forward as part of building trust within the team and enabling team dynamics

Pride: Intersection of People & their Intellectual property, gifts and expertise. Critical to get people on board as part of the team.

Strategic

Tactical

Process: In the context of team dynamics; Developing critical thinking, conflict management, powerful messaging & feedback

People: Mentoring individuals to Build Essential Skills, Mindset, Communication skills for impact and giving & receiving feedback.

Platform: also know as Tools needed in the context of human development and self management including: accountability, time management, decision Logic, Strategic planning skills

The CEO's Compass

Peace of Mind | Purpose | Performance | Past | Pride | Process | People | Platform

Case 3: Great Talent, Highly Engaged Workforce, But You're Still Herding Cats

Bring on the entrepreneurial spirit! This is what I find when an organization has talented people: everyone wants to work there, but they simply lack purpose to bring the strays together. This could also be said of the organization that still acts like a startup but has been around for 5-10 years and hasn't yet formulated a vision statement.

I love working with these companies because there is so much potential if we could just figure out what type of company they want to be when they grow up. I find these organizations can talk about the cool technology, amazing talent, and customers that are excited to work with them. But then they hit a wall and the business is not growing. Their current customers love them, but their new customers don't know what to make of them. And to make things worse, their employees cannot articulate the company purpose, and they're the closest to the customer.

Now, I'm not talking about brand marketing, and while that certainly helps, unless that sense of purpose and "who you are" as an organization is clearly seen, heard, and felt, the cats are going to run around your business—or in terms of the CEO's compass, the fish are flapping around on the deck! As evidence of this, I spoke to a few employees who worked at the company mentioned, and, while excited, they said there was a lot of chaos where structure was needed. Sound familiar? This is what happens when the company does not have a well-articulated purpose for people to align to. Investing a week or month may be all you need to remove the expense of the chaos people are currently experiencing.

During discovery with a potential client, I discussed this insight with the CEO, and they couldn't have agreed more. No amount of business development, R&D investments, or marketing would truly solve the problem until the leader set the purpose across all facets of the business.

You know what's coming next by now—I ask you a question! Think about your company, your team, or even yourself: is the purpose clearly communicated and (even more important) received? Receiving the message and demonstrating comprehension to align with that purpose is a leading indicator that you're getting back on track. That purpose aligned with performance will get you to peace of mind.

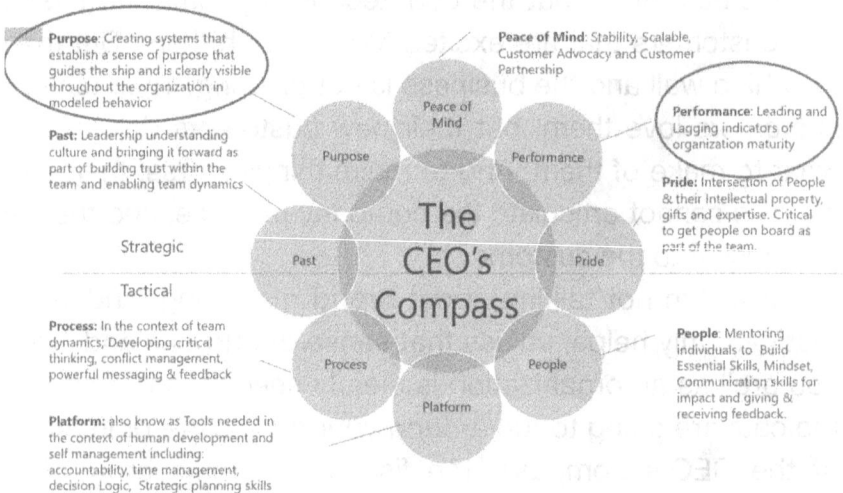

Purpose: Creating systems that establish a sense of purpose that guides the ship and is clearly visible throughout the organization in modeled behavior

Past: Leadership understanding culture and bringing it forward as part of building trust within the team and enabling team dynamics

Strategic

Tactical

Process: In the context of team dynamics; Developing critical thinking, conflict management, powerful messaging & feedback

Platform: also know as Tools needed in the context of human development and self management including: accountability, time management, decision Logic, Strategic planning skills

Peace of Mind: Stability, Scalable, Customer Advocacy and Customer Partnership

Performance: Leading and Lagging indicators of organization maturity

Pride: Intersection of People & their Intellectual property, gifts and expertise. Critical to get people on board as part of the team.

People: Mentoring individuals to Build Essential Skills, Mindset, Communication skills for impact and giving & receiving feedback.

The CEO's Compass

Peace of Mind

Purpose

Performance

Past

Pride

Process

People

Platform

Build the foundation right for your employees and your customers. Build it right and your business will last generations. Build it wrong and you're only a distant memory.

CHAPTER 12

Leaving a Lasting Impact and Handing the Compass to Your Team

While this brings me to the end of *The CEO's Compass*, it's really a beginning for you and your business, your team, or your career. I have shared the best of my experience to get leaders and myself back on track. I've asked you a lot of questions and, most importantly, I hopefully got you to think about what you need to get back on track. Through the actionable tips and tools I've shared with you, you have all that you need to go back to your situation and put a plan in place.

Nothing I've shared is rocket science, just a framework I've seen applied to countless situations that ultimately draws on the best that you have to offer. It's a tool, it's a guide, and it's the compass that with a few course corrections can get you back on track. You're already talented, and you can find the answers within yourself. It's simply a matter of going to your whiteboard, jotting down your thoughts, and letting them speak to you with your compass in your hand.

One More Story Before We Part Ways

In the early chapters of this book, I started to share with you my story of creating *The CEO's Compass* while I was in the throes of my own leadership journey and trying to get my team back on track. As you recall, there was no strategy except one that was cascaded down from corporate. My region was not performing well, and after self-reflection, I was able to create the Framework of One, my purpose, and the enabling structure and resources to move my ship from fourth place to ultimately second by the relevant performance metrics.

So, anticipating the next question (remember what I told you in Chapter 1: I see you!), here are the compass points I had to work on.

Purpose: There was an organizational purpose, but I had to create one for my region that resonated with our unique challenges. It also meant creating a roadmap for aligning each of my managers to the purpose so they were executing 70 percent of their time on activities that were moving the organization forward.

Performance: While achieving performance objectives of the organization were how we got our reviews and bonuses, I established a structure of monthly 1-2-1s with the team to align all of our roadmaps and leverage each other's support. These monthly 1-2-1s were mostly based on the difference between essential skills and technical skills; we also had weekly staff meetings for barrier removal. My job every day, week, and month was to remove barriers and elevate the performance of my team.

People: I had amazing talent in people who nonetheless had limiting mindsets, believe it or not. They only saw themselves as they had been judged based on past performance and could not see who they were in the eyes of others. I saw un-tapped leadership potential that could be achieved by lever-aging their skills and passions and removing limitations. Once we helped them to see a future state by leveraging roadmaps aligned to the purpose, we started really making a difference not only in the business but in their individual confidence. I was told once by a mentee that if they could only gain back their confidence, the rest would be easy. I have to say, once I helped to unleash the potential in the people, it was okay that they were way smarter than me—they were running now!

The Next Chapter Is for You to Write

When you close this book and we're no longer having this conversation, what is the next chapter for you? Think about the topics that resonated with you and think about how you felt knowing they were the opportunities you needed to pursue. Do you feel confident that you have all you need to create a plan for yourself? Was the information intriguing, but you're not sure where to start? Do you have so much information and questions left unanswered that now you feel overwhelmed? Was this a good read, but doesn't apply to you ... but could apply to someone else who is off course?

This book is to help you or someone you know who is not on track and never had a compass or is following one that no longer works. What will you do next? Do you pull out your compass and take a look to see where it's taking you? Do you want to leverage some of the insights because it may be just what you need to get back on track? Is there someone you know who you'd like to give the compass to because they've lost their way and need a tool that can serve them now and in the future?

The decision is yours to leave a lasting impact on those you lead or the people whom you are developing to lead others. *The CEO's Compass—Your Guide to Get You Back on Track* is my gift to you to leave your legacy.

I wish you success in your journey, and if I can help you get back on track with *The CEO's Compass*, I sincerely thank you for trusting me to be your guide.

Be the drummer to set the beat. You have one life in which to leave your legacy. Follow the beat of others, and you'll sound like everyone else. Set the beat, and create a symphony for others to play your music for years.

Please find free resources for all 12 chapters at:
https://dropinceo.com/theceoscompass

About the Author

Deb Coviello is the founder of Illumination Partners LLC, a consulting, leadership development, and media company dedicated to serving CEOs and business leaders going through rapid change and elevating their teams. With over twenty years in the flavor and fragrance industry in quality and operational excellence, Deb has the ability to identify, assess, and solve issues that are preventing

Deborah A. Coviello
Founder of Illumination Partners,
LLC and The Drop-in CEO

your business growth. Deborah also understands that people are the heart of your business. In order to deliver on her promise of offering you peace of mind, she focuses on utilizing the talents of your team, elevating them to new levels of performance, and setting them up to better serve your business.

When she isn't transforming businesses, Deborah hosts *The Drop-In CEO* podcast, mentors high performers, writes for numerous publications, and is an avid curler.

Deb has been married to her husband, Dan, for 33 years; she has three children Danny, David, and Sarah; a daughter-in-law, Camille; and one dog, Reagan, who keeps everyone on schedule.

Deb lives with her husband in Cincinnati, Ohio, but is a Jersey girl at heart!

You can reach Deb at deborah@coviellocm.com or https://dropinceo.com

www.ingramcontent.com/pod-product-compliance
Lightning Source LLC
Chambersburg PA
CBHW071651210326
41597CB00017B/2183